GLUCK, GLUCK, GLUCK.

Wine: an open-mouthed appreciation

MALCOLM GLUCK

with illustrations by Julia Whatley

BBC BOOKS

To Sue, for her wisdom,
love and tolerance –
and cooking

'"What did they live on?" said
Alice, who always took a
great interest in questions
of eating and drinking.'

LEWIS CARROLL, *Alice in Wonderland*

This book is published to accompany the television series
entitled *Gluck, Gluck, Gluck*
which was first broadcast in November 1996.
Executive producer Fiona Pitcher
Producer Tina Fletcher

Published by BBC Books,
an imprint of BBC Worldwide Publishing.
BBC Worldwide Limited, Woodlands,
80 Wood Lane, London W12 OTT
First published 1996

ISBN 0 563 37171 4

Illustrations by Julia Whatley
Set in Bembo
Printed and bound in Great Britain by Clays Ltd, St Ives plc
Cover printed by Clays Ltd, St Ives plc

CONTENTS

ACKNOWLEDGEMENTS

Without the *pyrotechnicienne* of Gaillac – and she must remain nameless – who lit the fuse, this book would never have exploded into existence. I thank her. I would also like to thank Nicky Copeland, Frank Phillips, Sarah Amit and Suzanne Webber of BBC Books – their enthusiasm was inspirational. Equally so has been the fervour with which their television counterparts, Fiona Pitcher, Tina Fletcher, Claudine Dabbs, Tony Moulsdale and Sharon Ward, have ploughed their side of the field. Felicity Rubinstein has my thanks, as usual; as do Linda Peskin, and Julia Whatley whose drawings enhance this book. I would also like to say to one special reader of my Weekend *Guardian* column, Michael Jackson, thank you for your faith and commitment

The publishers wish to acknowledge the following for permission to reproduce extracts from copyright material: Faber and Faber: *The Dead Sea Poems* by Simon Armitage; Jonathan Cape and the Estate of Bruce Chatwin: *Utz* by Bruce Chatwin; Penguin Books/Weidenfeld and Nicolson: *A Fan's Notes: A Fictional Memoir* by Frederick Exley; HarperCollins Publishers: *The Blue Flower* by Penelope Fitzgerald; Sinclair-Stevenson Publishers: *An Intimate History of Humanity* by Theodore Zeldin.

INTRODUCTION

'He is what he is, does whatever suits him,
because he has no highfalutin song
to sing.'
Simon Armitage, 'Goalkeeper with a Cigarette'
from The Dead Sea Poems, 1995

 This is a book about a revolution.
Or rather, it is a book about *two*
revolutions.

The one has followed so closely on the heels, or should I
say the dregs, of the other that we are scarcely conscious of
what has occurred. Nevertheless, these revolutions have spun,
they have been palpable and vivid, and they have changed the
way we live our lives.

The first revolution is the one which turned a nation of
bitter beer drinkers into a land of fruity wine lovers. Fifty
years ago just 4 per cent of Britons drank wine, and such
tipplers were strictly nobs. Nowadays, 70 per cent of us touch
the stuff.

I am not concerned here with how or why this has
happened – except to remark in passing that foreign holidays
and a greater interest in ethnic food and cooking are the
How, and the desire to break with the past and live more
healthily and roundly is the Why. My concern, and my
all-consuming, all-
swallowing concern,
is to look at the actual
wines themselves.

It is these wines
which are the fuel of
the second revolution. This revolution gave cheap wine
respectability both by making it well and making it widely

> **❛ My concern, my all-consuming,
> all-swallowing concern, is to look at the
> actual wines themselves. ❜**

available. The supermarkets' role here has been fundamental. Twenty years ago they were seen as mere purveyors of soap powder and cornflakes. Now they are Britain's leading wine merchants. The high street wine chains have responded to this challenge, with the result that this sceptred isle is now awash with plonk from fifty different countries, a far cry from the dozen or so favoured lands which supplied us in the early seventies.

Why is plonk respectable? Because the recession of the past few years has driven a vast number of drinkers, mainly men, to consider how they must more shrewdly finance their lifestyles. Money has become a commodity to be conserved, not to be chucked away without thought. Conspicuous consumption is seen, in the harsh light of the 1990s, as barbaric. Value for money is the new cry. Many cherished toys, and expensive habits, have been jettisoned. And the regular consumption of fancily priced wines was not a great hardship to forgo if there were deliciously fruity and very inexpensive alternatives on offer. The viciousness of the recession sanctioned these wines, and their popularity continues to grow; for they are not ersatz substitutes to endure in times of poverty but genuine articles to be enjoyed at any time – irrespective of the circumstances which might force the drinker to submit to the seductiveness of their prices.

Like so many cool oases at the edge of an uncomfortably

torrid desert the supermarkets have stood: open, unstuffy, mutely inviting. Men who regarded such emporia as unholy institutions thronged with housewives in curlers and carpet slippers; who thought of off-licences as dark caverns where Granny bought her Liebfraumilch and her chocolate bars; who thought the sun shone out of the undersides of bottles from the famous vineyard areas of the world – these men have changed their tunes. And with this new sweet music the second revolution proceeds full swing, giving a raw new impetus to the younger wine-producing countries and blowing the fresh wind of change through many of the less well-known vineyard areas of the Old World. The established pillars of wine are shaking.

It is an exciting time to drink wine, to make wine, to write about wine – new-style wine, that is, with its new-style fruitiness and astonishingly reasonable prices.

The old stylists are having a rough time of it. The old fogeys of the wine establishment and the entrenched European interests they serve are uncomfortable with the excitement generated by the new wines because they play little part in their production and a reluctant role in their consumption. The day of the English gentleman and his wine cellar piled high with claret, burgundy, hock, champagne and vintage port is gone. The vineyards which filled these cellars have only discovered a continuing economic basis for their existence, indeed a new wealth altogether in some instances, because of new post-1960s markets for expensive wine amongst the wine collectors and wine buffs of the USA and the new techno-millionaires in Japan and the Pacific Rim, as well as the long-established, well-heeled customers in Germany, northern Italy and Scandinavia, and, of course, those diehards in the UK who still revere the name on the label above the quality of the fruit in the bottle. It is important for such collectors, some of whom may also be drinkers, that the wine they buy *is* terribly expensive. The social and psychological returns for paying out an horrendous sum for

the liquid of pressed grapes are highly prized. If it could be guaranteed that every grape was personally crushed under the foot of the *vigneron*, instead of a Bucher press doing the dirty work, then I have no doubt that these collectors would cough up even vaster and more horrendous sums, regardless of whether the wine itself was one whit better.

I grew up, as a wine lover, on these Old World wines. I drank the last bottle of afford-able great burgundy to have been liquidized by feet, a Richebourg made by a man called Jean Gros, a few days before children arrived in my life and presented me with other priorities. My children will not drink these Old World wines. I may mourn this fact, wishing I could still buy a wonderfully gamy bottle of truffle-scented Nuits-St-Georges for thirty bob from the wine shop on the corner, but what is to be done? Indeed, what *should* be done?

Nothing. Let us enjoy the feast which is before us and celebrate the fruitier, healthier, less unstable and far more affordable wines of today. Let the revolution take its course.

This book is a catalogue of the bottled leaders of this revolution. But it is not a dry listing, for I have tried to convey also my deep love and enthusiasm for wine. I know of no more entertaining and, I hope, instructive way of doing this than by taking you the reader with me on my many travels, along the routes I have trodden and through the vineyards I have seen or dreamed about. I have also felt at liberty to introduce you to some of the motley bunch of characters who make and sell the wines I admire so much, for wine at bottom is a sensual experience before anything else, and its human side is most revealing. Wine is not manufactured to be written about as the scientific expression of a particular grape variety. Many writers on the subject do of course adopt this approach, but it is, at its best, only of interest to those for whom wine is a profession and, at its far more widespread worst, mere fodder for the wine snob who finds in pontification about vintages and analyses of microclimates the confirmation of wine's status symbolism.

I can assure you that not so many years ago the idea that such a book as this could be written – a book based on a TV series, no less – would have been laughed at as a fanciful impossibility by those incorrigible stick-in-the-muds who man the crumbling ramparts of the old wine establishment.

This laughter, as hollow as the pretension behind it, is in direct line of descent from the derision which would have greeted the proposition that one day Pinot Noirs from Romania, Shirazes from Australia, Sauvignon Blancs from New Zealand, Cabernet Sauvignons from Chile, Chardonnays from South Africa, Grenaches from Languedoc–Roussillon, Tempranillos from Valdepenas and Penedes in Spain, and Negroamaros from Puglia on Italy's heel, would one day be a common sight on the shelves of every high street wine retailer.

> **6 Wine… is a sensual experience before anything else, and its human side is most revealing. 9**

We are told that we live in a world which is shrinking daily. The modern wine drinker, in contrast, inhabits a world where the very opposite is true. As a result, someone in my line of work can find a valid excuse to be somewhere else in the world every other day of the week. I long ago gave up the habit of carefully returning to the bank my unspent pesetas, francs and Australian dollars. Who knows when I might suddenly need them?

A wine writer travels constantly. So he becomes something of a travel writer. A wine writer is constantly exposed to meals of every conceivable type, style, and nationality. So he also becomes a food writer. A wine writer meets all sorts of people. So he develops further into a bit of an anthropologist and social observer. And a wine writer must write to be read. So he must try to be something of an entertainer.

Of course, many a wine writer is nothing more than a writer about wine and finds the subsidiary details of the professional life of little significance. But I am as interested in them as I am in wine. Indeed, in many respects I regard wine as a mere accompaniment to those other things (meals, a good book, and human companionship especially). Fascinating as I find the technical aspects of a wine-maker's approach to his or her fermentation techniques I am equally interested – since she is, say, an Australian working in Bordeaux – in winkling out her views on how she finds being a foreign woman employed in an area of traditionally entrenched male chauvinism. Since this investigation can also be carried out in concert with another, like, for instance, the

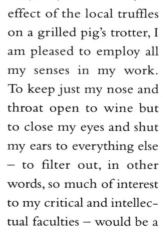

effect of the local truffles on a grilled pig's trotter, I am pleased to employ all my senses in my work. To keep just my nose and throat open to wine but to close my eyes and shut my ears to everything else – to filter out, in other words, so much of interest to my critical and intellectual faculties – would be a deprivation almost as great as having no wine in my glass.

In this book, therefore, although each essay involves a particular well-liked, perhaps even revered wine, or wines, you will not find a confused jumble, as in hotch-potch, but a patchwork of individually striking components which make up an ordered whole. I considered subtitling this Introduction 'Vaudeville among the Vines' because I invariably find trips overseas to meet wine-makers and tour vineyards totally absorbing and more often than not entertaining. I am rarely bored. Usually, I am constantly diverted and amused. It is not, I hope, absurdly ambitious of me to expect the reader of this book to feel likewise.

Does the word hotchpotch, unlike the organized but variegated patchwork to which I aspire in these pages, come directly from the German *hoch-pot* (a large cooking vessel into which many ingredients are tossed to make a family meal)? Does it originate from the French word *hocher* (which means to toss)? Or does it stem from *hâche en poche* (a sack of various edibles chopped up)? Years ago, it referred in Middle English directly to a multi-layered pudding composed of many spices and sweetmeats. In legal parlance, hotchpotch has a precise meaning: it is the collation into one whole of the various properties left by an intestate parent so that the surviving relatives may be bequeathed equal parts.

PLEASE READ THIS HEALTH WARNING BEFORE PROCEEDING FURTHER

There is no such thing as great wine, a reflective Frenchman once observed, there are only great bottles of wine. He meant that different bottles of the same wine, drunk at different times in different circumstances, may taste different, for better or worse, because wine changes over time, just as we humans do. However, such contrariness is insignificant compared to the difference between vintages of the same wine from the same vineyard.

I tell you this because some of the wines described in this book will undoubtedly be subject to vintage changes since I first tasted them and wrote about them. The wine world we now live in does not have one harvest time, which is our autumn; it has two, and new vintages of wines are coming on to the market all year round. During a British spring Australians, Chileans and New Zealanders are harvesting grapes which will become wine, some of which will go on sale just as European wine-growers are harvesting their crop of the same year. It is impossible, therefore, in a book like this, to guarantee that every single wine is exactly the same vintage as published. I tell you all this so that you may avoid losing your sanity or having an apoplectic fit when you cannot lay your hands on exactly the bottle you're after. If I rave about or condemn a wine of a particular vintage, there is absolutely no reason on earth why the wine of the next vintage will be even a distant cousin, let alone a close relative.

> **❛ There is always a difference between wines of a different vintage from the same vineyard. ❜**

Of course, part of a wine-maker's skill is to apply oenological techniques which minimize the shortcomings of a particular vintage, but miracles are beyond any oenologist.

Blending skills are not, though. By meticulously blending different tanks or barrels of wine, which may be all one grape variety or a mix of several, any discernible difference between wines of succeeding vintages may represent a raising of quality, not a lowering of it. This happy state is not always reached, however. Not only that – two wines bearing precisely the same label except for a small change in the date of vintage may be neither better nor worse but merely different. One of the stupidest myths in wine is that vines in hot, sunny countries create fewer differences in the wines they ultimately produce because the weather is always clement. This is utter tripe. There is *always* a difference between wines of a different vintage from the same vineyard, just as there are differences in style and weight of fruit in different batches of blended non-vintage wines. With these latter wines, like, say, Romanian Pinot Noir (more of this on pages 48–52), these differences will be less overtly conspicuous if the winery blenders are mustard-hot and able to call on a consistent supply of past vintages over two or three years old which can always be used with younger wines to provide a regular supply of a blend which is habitually of a similar quality. But even here there is no guarantee.

Equally, I cannot guarantee that all the prices given in this book will be the same to the exact penny as when I wrote them down. Lastly, I cannot even guarantee that all the wines I have described within these pages will still be on sale at the retailers stated. Although the retailers of the most prominent wines were confident that they would still be stocking them as you read this, there is no guarantee that later vintages have not replaced older ones. Some of the wines mentioned here and there in the text, certain of which I have drooled over, may now be but a memory. What control have I over time? In between my words hitting the page and the book hitting the shelves, stocks of a particular wine may become exhausted. The retailer may decide not to sell the next vintage; he may dislike the new wine or find it too dissimilar from the previous vintage to appeal. He may not be able to buy it if the new vintage is of such low yield that supplies are restricted. Wine is a hostage to several fortunes (weather being even more uncertain and unpredictable than exchange rates), but the wine writer is hostage to just one: he cannot pour for his readers precisely the same wine as he poured for himself.

Downright Unfair Comparisons

(Also Odious, Odorous, Offensive, and Utterly Ludicrous)

I t is often remarked that it is totally unfair to compare a three-quid bottle of wine with one costing two or three times that sum (or even, as we shall see, one costing twenty times as much). And I entirely agree. But not for the reasons you might expect.

Many more times than you would believe credible, more expensive bottles simply don't stand a chance when they are compared with their cheaper brethren. To be sure, sometimes the pricier bottle may be more concentrated, occasionally it may possess a distinct bouquet, but not only may its overall fruitiness compare unfavourably with the less expensive wine, often it is not so engaging a companion when drunk with

food. And it is with food, after all, that wine is designed to go. I am also regularly disappointed by pricey bottles as companions for solo pursuits like listening to music or reading a book. The hollowness of the wine soon palls and, when that price tag sits up and starts wagging its noughts at you and interrupts the plot or the poem, I find myself irritated that yet another much-vaunted bottle is a wimp.

The pleasure a wine provides, unless you are so spoiled by wealth that you possess no moral ready reckoner with which to compute value for money (or you are too reckless or indiscriminating in taste to care), is surely related to its price. This is not, I concede, a smooth mathematical correlation. I do not expect a wine costing £100 to be exactly ten times better than one costing £10, or twenty times better than one costing a fiver, but does it not seem reasonable to expect there to be a significant difference in the quality of two wines so differentiated in price?

> ❛ The pleasure a wine provides ... is surely related to its price. ❜

With so many expensive wines, it comes down to the impression the buyer wishes to create, not the quality he wants to acquire. Is a Ferrari at £100,000 a more reliable mode of transport than a Toyota at £10,000? I rather doubt it. I cannot turn heads in the Toyota and excite young men and women, and I cannot reach 150 mph in the cheaper vehicle, but if my sole object is to travel from A to B, then this is achieved without fuss. For me, the purpose of wine is not to turn heads but to provide perfect enjoyment, reliability and satisfaction en route from A (the pocket) to B (the palate). 'You boring old fart, what a lot of excitement you are giving up,' do I hear you mutter? In fact, the only excitement I am losing out on is the expenditure of a great deal of money.

I am forced to conclude, after giving wine and its price a great deal of thought, that the sensuality of fruit that I seek to find in wine is, when it is missing in an expensive bottle, compensated for only by a sky-high price. Is the laying out of a great deal of money on wine a sensual experience in itself? For many men it would appear so: a wine *is* sensual because it costs a fortune to acquire. Posh and costing lots of dosh are irresistible features of a wine bottle, it would seem. There can be no other reason for the trade in expensive wine, which is male-dominated — in terms of both buying and selling — to a huge degree. It is a silly and immature practice. But then no man, as a Chinese sage remarked, is so mature that death cannot come along and make him more so.

Playing the Comparisons Game

Let us compare a bottle of **Chateau Brane-Cantenac 1981** (T&W Wines of Thetford in Norfolk, £24.38) with **El Liso Barrel-Aged Tempranillo 1993** (Victoria Wine, £3.99). The first wine is a Margaux, a fancied wine ranked in the Bordeaux classification system devised in 1855, and still in operation today, as a *deuxième cru classé*. Not quite of the Ferrari rank, then, but certainly a top-of-the-range BMW or Mercedes in price nevertheless. El Liso is a Spanish red made by Californian Ed Flaherty in the La Mancha wine region which, like Conca de Barbera in Tarragona in northern Spain (discussed more fully in Chapter 6), has no international reputation whatsoever. El Liso is a bottom-of-the-range Honda pricewise. Shall we compare the **Backsberg Merlot 1993** (Tesco, £4.99) from South Africa with the same store's **Les Forts de Latour Bordeaux**

Comparisons are Odious

1985 (£25.99)? Or what of **Echezeaux Grand Cru Paul Dugenais 1993** (Sainsbury, £18.95) with **Romanian Special Reserve Pinot Noir 1990** (Morrison, the northern supermarket chain, £3.35)? **Fortant de France Domaine d'Aubian Chardonnay Vin de Pays d'Oc 1994** (Sainsbury, £4.25) with **Corton Charlemagne Louis Latour 1993** (Majestic Wine Warehouses, £34.50)?

The game is virtually infinite. We can play it with thousands of wines in thousands of combinations. And we shall discover that unless a drinker has had his grey cells addled and is completely barmy, then the difference in the wines is not remotely large enough to make the difference in price sane or even reasonable. In my book, even when the difference is in the more expensive wine's favour and sufficiently pronounced to register on the taste-buds, it is rarely a difference worth paying for.

Sometimes the difference in price is so outrageous when compared with the difference in pleasure (with the cheaper wine always winning) that it defies belief. In the autumn of 1995 I invited an acquaintance of mine to take away some red and white burgundies, varying in price between £13 and £70 and which I had already sampled and tasted, to use in a blind tasting (that is to say, the bottles were disguised so that no one would know from which bottle a particular wine came). My acquaintance also took with him a bottle of Bulgarian wine costing £3. When the group of drinkers, including so-called wine buffs, were invited to guess which wine was which, the most expensive, an Aloxe-Corton, was taken to be the £2.99 Bulgarian, and the £2.99 Bulgarian

was thought to be the pricey French wine.

But what of the wines I have made a particular point of comparing above? How do they compare, sip with sip? Let me go through them.

Chateau Brane-Cantenac 1981 *versus* El Liso Barrel-Aged Tempranillo 1993

There is some aromatic enticement about both wines, and the Bordeaux certainly suggests riches to be discovered. But where the Spanish fruit is giving and warm and delicious, the French fruit is reluctant, a touch tight, and not especially deep or thrilling. There is simply much more sensuality and companionability with the Tempranillo. Texturally it is smooth, yet not so highly polished that its character is obscured. The Bordeaux is grumpy and does not exhibit any great smoothness of manner with the appropriate food (roast lamb). Overall, the Brane-Cantenac is dull. El Liso is much more spirited company.

Backsberg Merlot 1993 *versus* Les Forts de Latour Bordeaux 1985

The Cape wine gushes with flavour and has a leather-tinged bouquet which is fully realized in the fruit. Caressingly velvety and purposeful, it strides on to the palate where the Bordeaux limps. True, there is some suggestion of a commanding aroma with the more expensive wine, but it doesn't seem willing to release the fruit you *imagine* must lie behind it. The finish is cheap and somewhat grudging. The Cape wine bends over backwards to please.

Echezeaux Grand Cru Paul Dugenais 1993 *versus* Romanian Special Reserve Pinot Noir 1990

Both wines are made from the same grape but they are a world apart in flavour and vigour. The Echezeaux offers some hint of the vegetal classiness which is its trademark when you smell the wine, but even here the Romanian cheapie is more inviting and farmyardy. The fruit in the French wine is little above ordinary; the other wine has depth and flavour and a lingering finish.

Fortant de France Domaine d'Aubian Chardonnay Vin de Pays d'Oc 1994 *versus* Corton Charlemagne Louis Latour 1993

Beautifully textured, deep, balanced, handsomely well-finished and even a bit luxurious. But which wine? The first one, of course. Why is the Latour wine so much less satisfying and less of an exciting expression of the same Chardonnay grape? I can't tell you. I can only comment as I find, and what I find is that where the first wine is stealthy, witty, charming and stylish, the second wine is gawky, witless, ill-poised and outrageously over-priced.

It would not be difficult for me to find hundreds of similar examples, but I will rest my case with the assertion that all the wines which I enthuse about in this book, and many of these cost under a fiver, are considerably more interesting and considerably better value than literally thousands of wines which cost many times more. Often the comparison can be made with wines not produced thousands of miles apart but separated by a few hills. I think, for example, that the red Bordeaux at Sainsbury by the name of **Vieux Chateau Landon 1990**, from the Médoc (the *bas*, or low, Médoc as it happens), and which costs under £9, is considerably better as a wine, and a huge improvement in terms of value for money, than many of the world-famous wines from the *haut*, or high, Médoc. And in a similar neighbourly paradox I find many of the famous white wines of Burgundy

> ❛ … all the wines which I enthuse about in this book, and many of these are under a fiver, are considerably more interesting and considerably better value than literally thousands of wines which cost many times more. ❜

not as interesting, at anything from £30 to £100, as one of the **Macon Blanc Villages** made by **Domaine des Deux Roches** which can be found at around £7 at Oddbins and Fullers wine shops in the London area.

Later on in this chapter we will also see that to compare a bottle of the legendary Chateau Latour with a Californian Reserve Cabernet from Robert Mondavi, is to discover that the American wine is superior. And, from the same State and in the same state of mind, to compare the fruit in a wine like Ridge Paso Robles Zinfandel (the most expensive subject of an encomium in these pages at around £15 a bottle and the star of Chapter 13) even with one containing an example of the most expensive liquids of French, Italian or Spanish vineyards – that is to say, wines costing three and four times as much – is not to compare like with like in any way, shape or form. The Zinfandel, to my mind and taste–buds, would stand out clearly as a far more exciting wine: more sensual, more aromatically vigorous, deeper and more richly endowed with complexity and breadth of flavour, and able to handle a wider variety of robustly flavoured foods. Fifteen pounds is a lot of money (I reckon no wine, unless it's an antique rarity, should cost much more than this – it's only the same price as a newly published hardback novel after all). Fifty or sixty quid is a fortune. But if you're going to take £15 out of your pocket you should expect from the wine you buy something which enhances your life and adds a dimension to it (like the hardback novel), not only during the time the wine has actually lasted in the glass and impinged directly on your senses, but afterwards as a deliciously sharp memory, a rousing sensual experience as vividly recalled as the first time you heard something by Schumann delicately issuing from the piano, or when you got so close to the boy or girl next door that you felt your shoes would melt. I do not say that no French, Italian or Spanish wine offers this experience (indeed, Chapter 6 reveals how one Spanish wine became, in a comparative tasting organized by the French, the most highly regarded wine of all), only that if high price alone is taken as a guaranteed criterion of excellence, deep disappointment will result.

The game of Odious Comparisons is not one which only drinkers alert to value for money can play. The game's biggest devotees are often the wineries; for wine-makers delight in comparing their own wines with the world's so-called best. When the comparison is favourable, you can bet your last penny-piece I get to hear about it.

> ❛ ... if high price alone is taken as a guaranteed criterion of excellence, deep disappointment will result. ❜

AN ENLIGHTENING (AND LIGHTNING) TRIP TO PUGLIA: COPERTINO RISERVA, £3.99 *VERSUS* ROMANEE-ST-VIVANT, £70

'Every month a tanker arrives, fills up, and drives to the Côte d'Or. Our wine makes first class Appellation Contrôlée burgundy, don't you agree?'

The above quote, taken from a conversation I had with an executive of the wine co-operative from which Sainsbury buys its splendid Copertino Riserva (and passes on to its customers at under a fiver a bottle), amounts to a major wine scandal, if the man's claim is even remotely true. I have no shred of circumstantial evidence to enable me to discover whether this is so, and less interest in doing so. I am much more intrigued at the *presumption* behind the claim. I rather think the Italian had forgotten I was a journalist when he passed the remark in his exuberant English. And even had he used his even more exuberant Italian, he would not have been misunderstood because I was in the company of Sainsbury's wine buyer, Mark Kermode, a man who spent his boyhood in Rome and speaks the language as if born to it (though he often conceals this fact during buying negotiations with Italian suppliers, for obvious reasons).

Puglia

The idea that wine could be transported from the heel of Italy to the crown of Burgundy in order for the one to bolster the other is a great compliment to the original vines. The revelation that the practice might exist was made not to encourage me to run to the authorities, or to write about the perfidious French and their willingness to cheat; it was made to prove that this Copertino's excellence and worth were sanctioned by the highest authority of all: the great Appellation Bourgogne Contrôlée. For the bureaucrats behind this authority, the INAO as it is called, were prepared to tolerate the deception just as surely as they knew that it went on. And why should they not tolerate it? All that would be involved would be a simple transference of liquid from one brother in wine to another. How else could certain burgundies, I was invited to believe, maintain their level of richness in poor vintages (or even in so-called normal good ones) when the fruit was meagre except by calling on the wines of their sunnier neighbour?

Wines from one region, or another country altogether, which are used to bolster wines from another, are called *vins du médecin* – not in reference to the healthy level of tannin and warm fruit they might flaunt but because they are used, as were cheap Algerian and Rhône wines in the past, to 'doctor' wines of wealthier regions able to demand a higher price for their bottles. It is an utterly illegal practice. A wine which says Appellation Something Contrôlée on its label must come from the Something region, which is strictly demarcated by wine law. The smaller the Appellation referred to – Nuits-St-Georges, say, rather than the more all-encompassing Bourgogne – the tougher and tighter the restrictions on the area with regard to exactly where the wine is grown.

All this was irrelevant to the man from Copertino. He said what he said to impress me. And as such it was an interesting clue to his confused mentality and his typically Italian, highly ambiguous scorn for authority on the one hand yet his deference to it on the other. Had he known how little regard I have for burgundy generally as a wine, and the contempt in which I hold *appellation* laws as instruments for maintaining excellence and quality, he might have thought again. But then again he might not. In his eyes it was inconceivable that anyone could not be impressed by his statement, whether true or not, that his wine was employed by a neighbouring wine-growing nation to deepen the flavour of a wine internationally regarded as one of the planet's greatest.

Such is Copertino, made largely from the Negroamaro grape. It is a deep, sturdy, mature red, dry, husky and richly fruity with undertones of coffee and tobacco (all smoothed out as a result of its oak-aging). It is an old leather armchair of a wine in some respects. Burgundy is made from Pinot Noir, and only rare examples exhibit some of the vinous properties just ascribed to Copertino. Yet how many so-called connoisseurs have been drinking the Pinot Noir blended with the Copertino, thinking it was a 100 per cent burgundy and paying a handsome price for the privilege? I cannot say. A fool and his money are soon parted.

How does Copertino stand up to expensive burgundies? Well, all I can tell you is that last autumn Majestic Wine Warehouses sent me some mind-bogglingly pricey examples from négociant Louis Latour, and I felt none of them had the edge on the Copertino. The Italian wine was silkier and more savoury and altogether more pungent company for food. Yet this is a wine, don't forget, which retails under £4. It felt more agreeable on nose and in throat than **Beaune Vignes Franches 1986** at £12.99, and even Latour's £70 bottle of **Romanee-St-Vivant**, which had some real texture to its fruit, struggled to match the enticing mouthful which was the Copertino. Evidence, if nothing else, that Latour remains faithful to the local vines for all their fruit but, sadly in my view, also evidence that such wines are routinely pasteurized prior to bottling. This practice, which confers a desirable stability on the wines but also subtracts from their character and typicity, is stifling individuality and cramping style and, if such things mean anything in relation to such high-priced status symbols, destroys any basis they might have as fine wines even if they possessed any fineness before being pasteurized (which I doubt). As objects upon which a value-for-money assessment might be bestowed, such wines defy sensible classification in the way that a male stripper could claim to be a dramatic actor only by an extreme stretch of the imagination.

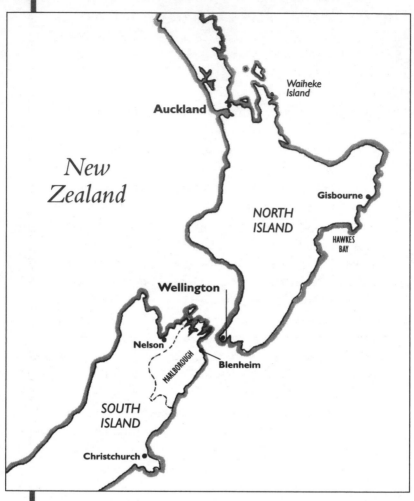

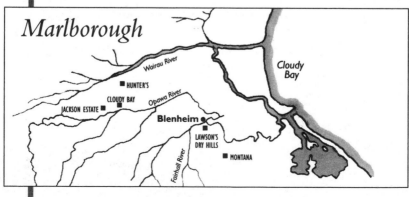

DANNY BROWN, FRENCHMAN BY BIRTH, NEW ZEALANDER BY REBIRTH: DANIEL LE BRUN SPARKLING WINE VERSUS THE FINEST MARQUES OF CHAMPAGNE

'*The first settlers were sheepfarmers but most of them found that sheepfarming interfered too much with racing and they were forced to retire and live nearer the course.*' C.V. Smith, *A Humorous Survey of New Zealand*, 1947

Climate was one reason why Daniel Le Brun emigrated to New Zealand twenty years ago. Or, rather, settled in one specific region of the country: Marlborough. This titular homage is not to the world's biggest-selling cigarette but to John Churchill, first Duke of Marlborough. Whether Daniel felt any qualms about moving to a spot named after an English soldier who thrashed the Frogs something rotten in four great eighteenth-century battles over five years – Blenheim, Ramillies, Oudenarde and Malplaquet – he did not say. I rather doubt he gave a *figue*. The climate and the soil were perfect for his purposes and that is what mattered.

Certainly the benevolent autumnal sun beamed on Danny's vineyard and wine buildings the day I met him. He was wearing denim shorts cut very short and on his head sat a cap with a strawberry emblem. It is possible that had he been

presenting his sparkling wines to me in his native Champagne instead of his adopted country he would have worn an Armani suit with an art deco tie or perhaps a Jean-Louis Gaultier ensemble. But ignore his dress sense. Consider his name. He really needs to change it to Danny Brown. What sort of phony-sounding moniker is Le Brun? How could such a name be found on such wondrous sparkling wine? Fortunately, this has not deterred several retailers from stocking **Daniel Le Brun Brut** and these include Tanners of Shrewsbury, Booths of Preston, and Lea and Sandeman in London. Harrods and Fortnum and Mason also stock the wine, thus somewhat contradicting the belief that bargains are unknown at these emporia. For in spite of Danny's brut non-vintage fizz costing around twelve quid or less, it is one of the classiest sparkling wines you will ever encounter – at any price. It possesses that rare but highly prized attribute: the elegant fruit to charm along with the soothing acidity to seduce. It is delicate yet rich; the mousse is soft; there is a delicious, subtly peachy edge to the fruit. It rates almost as high in my estimation as a sparkling wine can. The only bubbly which pips it is Alain Robert's great blended non-vintage masterpiece, **Les Mesnil**, which is only sold in the Champagne region itself and through a few selected outlets in other parts of France, and costs around seventy quid – yes £70 – a bottle.

'Only in the very best years in Champagne,' said Monsieur Le Brun, 'would I be able to make a sparkling wine this good.' He is being extremely polite and patriotic, loyal and sentimental; very few champagnes ever taste as invigoratingly delicious as his sparkling wine, whatever the vintage or price. The pity is how little he makes: 130,000–140,000 bottles at most in a good year. The Champagne region as a whole turns out 300 million bottles in any year, good, bad or indifferent.

Other sparkling wines made in the Marlborough region also demonstrate great flair and flavour. These include **Nautilus NV Brut** (Majestic Wine Warehouses, £10.49); **Pelorus** (around £13 at Adnams, Lea and Sandeman, Harrods, Selfridges, Harvey Nichols and others), which is made by the same gifted crowd who turn out the gooseberry-intense **Cloudy Bay Sauvignon Blanc** (upwards of a tenner at Majestic Wine Warehouses, Wine Rack, Oddbins, Fullers, Davisons, Lay and Wheeler, Adnams, Avery's, Tanners,

Corney and Barrow, Berry Bros. and Rudd, plus at least twelve other London merchants and some four dozen provincial ones); and **Jane Hunter's 1991** Brut of which only fifty cases found their way to England, to go down the gullets of the incredibly lucky, and exceedingly well-heeled, clientele of the restaurant at 21 Queen Street, Newcastle where it appears on the wine list at twenty-six quid – or did when this book went to press, but with Newcastle producing the sort of football they are currently playing, I suspect that delirious fans have long since consumed the lot. The well-known **Montana Lindauer Brut** is the cheapest of these Marlborough bubblies (Sainsbury, £6.75; Tesco, £6.79) and this wine offers delicious drinking and very good value.

NEW ZEALAND SAUVIGNON BLANCS AND CHARDONNAYS VERSUS EACH OTHER

John and Warwick Stitchbury do not own a winery as such and so I was asked to taste their **Jackson Estate Sauvignon Blanc** (Tesco, Waitrose and Oddbins, £7.99) at the top of a weather-station watchtower in the middle of their vineyard, situated in Marlborough's Wairau Valley, while the brothers slid open windows and pulled on fags. This station registers information on a half-hour basis and is connected to an electronic alarm beside John Stitchbury's bed. If frost threatens, the alarm goes off and, if necessary, he can immediately call up a helicopter to fly to the vineyard where the action of its blades disturbing the air will drive cold air upwards and bring the warmer air down. This is indeed a high-tech vineyard. And it has turned out some wonderful wine.

Vertigo, I promise you, was not responsible for the delirious condition in which I emerged from this watchtower after tasting Jackson Estate wines, for the vintages I sampled were all persuasively fruity, high-rating examples of scrumptious complexity. The actual wine-making is done by a local contract winery, Rapara Vintners, and the wine-maker is Australian Martin Shaw who keeps in regular touch via a fax machine and in irregular personal touch via flying visits to both vineyard and winery.

Jackson Estate wines are among the more expensive ones to be made by a flying wine-maker. The purists who imagine that great wine can only be made by a full-time, barefoot, fusspot octogenarian who kips in an old barrel in the corner of the  cellar with a yellow Gauloise permanently gummed to his lower lip, a flea-bitten slouch which was once a gundog slinking behind him, find the Stitchbury style an itch they can't scratch (and as unnerving as the royal red telephone box that sits at the end of a row of their vines and from which no phone calls are ever made, only calls of nature). Here, among the Stitchbury vines and especially tasting the Stitchbury wines (all called Jackson Estate in one grape form or another because, according to John, 'We couldn't call it Stitchbury so we called it Jackson after Jackson Road where the vineyard is, which is also Mum's maiden name'), it dawns upon the visitor exactly what the secret of great Sauvignon Blanc is – indeed, what is the very secret of the wonderful fruit the whole New Zealand wine industry produces.

The secret is that the climate naturally produces cool nights and hot days plus a very long ripening season. The daytime sun creates grape sugars, the nights develop the acids, and the unusually lengthy time the grapes spend on the vines allows these two essential elements of sugar and acid to marry more cogently and expressively. The result, aided and abetted by shrewd viticultural techniques, some of which, like new ideas on what is called 'canopy management' (a technique that develops the relationship between the vine leaves and the bunches of grapes and organizes it to produce a finer crop), and a better understanding of how to handle the resultant grapes to produce the best balance in the finished wine, is some wonderful, world-class bottles. This is especially true of the Marlborough region, made famous among wine buffs a mere eleven years ago when the first Marlborough Sauvignon Blanc, **Cloudy Bay**, burst on to the palates of wine drinkers. If the length of the growing season suits this kind of grape, in Marlborough there is the added advantage of vineyard soil covered in large grey stones which play an invaluable role in retaining heat and reflecting it back up into the vines, even when the ambient air temperature is low.

At Jackson Estate, which has only been producing its wine under its own label since 1991 (and it was only a few years before this that the vineyard itself was planted, originally with the idea of merely selling all its output to wineries), there is an added incentive for the vines to develop extensive roots and find deep mineral sustenance: there is no irrigation. This is unusual. At neighbouring vineyards, even at Cloudy Bay's, there are irrigation pipes among the vines. (Which proves how astonishingly small a microclimate can be where vines are concerned; for here are two world-class vineyards only walking distance apart – a single kilometre to be exact – and one finds the need to irrigate and the other does not. It also demonstrates that irrigation, which in the eyes of many European vineyard owners is a heresy, is merely another technique to be mastered, for who can doubt the magnificent quality of Cloudy Bay's fruit?)

In spite of such a seemingly purist attitude to their vines, the Stitchburys (John manages the vines, Warwick runs the office) do not live to grow wine. They grow wine to live. Not for them a weekend spent cosseting every vine as if it were a child running a fever. 'We rather prefer to run down to the Bay and get on the boat and get the rods out. When you taste our salmon you'll taste salmon for the first time.' An hour after

John said this, I did get to enjoy this locally caught fish and I must admit that for flavour and texture it beat hollow any salmon I've ever eaten in Britain, or Canada for that matter. 'Different type of salmon. Different sort of ocean,' said Warwick. The richness of the fish went wonderfully well with the richness of the 1994 Sauvignon Blanc from Jackson Estate which accompanied it. Indeed, this wine provoked an astonishing reaction from a tourist when the Stitchburys and I walked into the

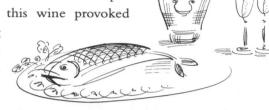

restaurant which provided the fish. At the sight of the Jackson Estate bottle with its distinctive gumtree on the label, a customer gasped, leaped up and rushed across.

'My God, you have Jackson Estate Sauvignon Blanc! Where did you get it? It's my favourite wine. Please tell me where you got it. I've come all the way from England to visit Jackson Estate and I can't find it. They don't even have a winery let alone a visitors' centre, so where can I buy the wine?' he beseeched in a ringing London accent.

The Stitchburys looked both pleased that their wine should provoke such a response and concerned that they were confronted by a complete nutter. I told the Londoner that after I had found out how the wine went with the salmon he could finish the remains of the bottle. He couldn't have beamed with more joy if he had just been handed a suspended sentence after being threatened with life imprisonment. When my meal was cut short ten minutes later by the arrival of a representative of another vineyard coming to whisk me off elsewhere, I left a very happy man with half a bottle of Jackson Estate '94. Whether this happy soul would have felt so ecstatic if he had had the 1995 Jackson Estate Sauvignon Blanc or the 1995 Chardonnay in front of him is open to question. Both these wines lacked the concentration and sheer voluptuousness of fruit of earlier vintages, and the finish on both was a touch wimpish. Certainly the Sauvignon is not in the class of the two finest Marlborough Sauvignons of 1995 – the limpid Cloudy Bay and the rich Goldwater Dog Point.

James and Annie Millton of the only certified organic vineyard in New Zealand, in Gisborne, have a closer relationship with their winery, for not only do they make all their own wine, they go to bed barely more than a cat's whisker away from the winery building itself. In their modern airy house overlooking the deep hunched banks of the Te Arai river, with wooden floors as well as wooden doors and windows which open generously to admit light and air, there appear to be no walls at all. The Milltons, with baby daughter Monique and Sam the dog, live the sort of arboreal existence which those of us cowering behind the solid bricks of a distant, noisy and polluted metropolis can only dream about. Sam catches pheasants which raid the vines. Annie can pull up a dozen varieties of herbs plus vegetables and orchard fruit (and olives, garlic, artichokes and various beans) from the garden in front of the kitchen. Monique can play safely in woods, on grass, in trees, and by the small swimming pool. And James has his vines. Safeway sometimes stocks **Millton Chardonnay/Semillon (£4.99)**, which is full of ripe fruit

with a delicate citrus finish and is a lovely aperitif as well as suiting delicate fish dishes. Vintage Roots (tel.: 01734 40122), a wine merchant specializing in organic wines, also stocks Millton wines and sells a Chenin Blanc and a Chardonnay (at around £7.50 and £8.99 respectively).

Most New Zealand Sauvignons and Chardonnays fit food as naturally as Larry Adler's mouth encloses a harmonica. This food can be smoked fish (salmon and eel), poached and grilled fillets of fish (sole, turbot, red mullet especially) and the whole gamut of crab, lobster, squid and shellfish dishes generally. The richer New Zealand Sauvignons are quite wonderful with the country's large green mussels done the Thai way with lemon grass. But some of the Chardonnays suit even sturdier and richer fare. **Delegats Oyster Bay Chardonnay**, costing around £8 at Sainsbury, will cope with chicken in black bean sauce. This is a beautifully concentrated wine with a creamy, woody texture shot through with tropical fruit acids. Delegats makes a whole variety of red and white wines, all masterminded by one of New Zealand's most talented wine-makers, Brent Marris, and they are gaining popularity with many of the major retailers as well as the smaller wine merchants.

Majestic Wine Warehouses and Fullers have in the past stocked the hugely attractive **Goldwater Chardonnay** (£8.89) made by Kim and Jeanette Goldwater who are based on Waiheke Island just across the bay from Auckland. They also produce wines in Marlborough made under contract. The Waiheke Island fruit, however, is a tribute not just to superior viticulture (helped by Waiheke's magnificent climate) but to clever wine-making.

Kim was once a civil engineer who helped build Imperial College in London's Queen's

> **'** Most New Zealand Sauvignons and Chardonnays fit food as naturally as Larry Adler's mouth encloses a harmonica. **'**

Gate and, like the Milltons, he's keen on the particular kind of open air New Zealanders breathe. 'Do you feel how clean it is here in this country?' he said to me when he took me on a tour of his Waiheke vines. 'That air didn't cross any continent to reach us. It just blew up from Antarctica.' It was Kim who demonstrated to me the old truth that every vine has its own microclimate; for as I tasted some of his grapes (on vines maybe five weeks from harvest), the difference between the ripeness levels of the same variety of grapes was wide, and between different varieties of grapes vast. Sauvignon Blanc: ripe and magnificently smoky. Cabernet Sauvignon: sweet with rapidly developing acidity. Merlot: already complex and fine. I also sampled Jeanette's gastronomic hospitality, based entirely on the garden around the vineyard or on produce grown locally: tortilla, tomato salad with feta cheese, ratatouille and home-baked bread, fresh macadamia nuts (the very devil to crack open).

Majestic also has the delightful **Coopers Creek Sauvignon Blanc** (under £7 and also at Victoria Wine). Thresher and its Wine Rack and Bottoms Up subsidiaries offer the elegant, unwooded **Selaks Sauvignon Blanc** for around £6. Sainsbury, in a mere twenty-five branches, had the superb **Matua Sauvignon Blanc** and **Chardonnay** of the 1994 vintage but these wines have long gone. The '95 vintage will be on sale when this book appears. If they are as good as the '94, these wines will be utterly beguiling. Both offer a torrent of deep, rich fruit which never for a moment slackens its grip or oversteps the mark to become unbalanced and blowsy (good words with which to nail overfruity wines of which one glass is more than enough).

There is often a delicacy of touch in New Zealand Sauvignons and particularly certain Chardonnays which is so thrilling that it is as devastating as a cross-court drop-shot on a tennis court when perfectly executed: deft, precise, crushing, concentrated. Many Rieslings are also excellent and would excite the most jaded and cynical palate fed up with stark Germans. The most wonderfully rich and complex Riesling I ever tasted was from Neil McCullum's Dry River vineyard. The wine's fruit had a whiplash of balancing acidity of stunning, mineralized intensity. It was one of those wines you could drink for ever, and the emptying of the last drop was mourned like the last day of a perfect holiday.

New Zealand Chardonnays have now and then achieved equally dramatic effects, particularly those of the Neudorf vineyard. The **1993 Moutere Chardonnay** from Neudorf, a vineyard and winery run by Tim and Judy Finn, was quite lovely. The notes, inscribed with a sober pen in a sober hand, which I made about this wine, having consumed as much as I dared of the bottle Tim Finn offered me as we sat on the back porch sipping (or rather he was sipping, I was fighting hard not to swallow), read as follows: '...gently smoky, toasty aroma – seductive, subtle, delicate fruit of great class, restrained power and great persistence – leaves an imprint on the tongue of having been caressed by a mysterious fruit which is a new mutation – a quietly stunning wine of elegance and purposefulness.' Sigh I might at the memory of it, for can you buy this wine in the UK? Adnams had the '92 at nigh on fifteen quid, and of the '93 Tim told me the Wine Society had just fifty cases, now all consumed (or lying in some lucky blighter's cellar somewhere, though he'd better not wait too long before drinking his treasure because a large part of the wine's charm was its youth). Other high-class wines from this vineyard also include Riesling and Sauvignon Blanc and that bug-bear, as far as I am concerned, Pinot Noir. I tasted the '94 just before this book went to press and it was wonderful, with an elegance and cool charm which defy description but encourage the drinker to believe he has utterly unique wine in his glass. The **Neudorf 1995 Sauvignon Blanc**, which was blended from local Nelson area fruit and fruit from Marlborough, I found less impressive.

Sadly, all these wonderful wines – the whiplash concentrated Sauvignons, the opulently fruity Chardonnays – add up to comparatively few bottles. In a good year like 1995, say, a mere 70,000 metric tons of New Zealand grapes will be harvested in the whole of the country. There are co-operative wineries in South Africa and Europe, and establishments in Australia, which crush the same amount of fruit annually on an individual basis. The Kiwis can boast just 200 or so wine producers (four of which account for nigh on 90 per cent of the total production) whereas in just one vineyard area of France, like Alsace, say, there are around 1800 producers out of a total of 7000–8000 individuals who own vineyards but sell their crop to a co-operative. In the seven months prior to January 1995, New Zealand exported 3.3 million litres of wine to the UK. This contributed to the country having something over 1 per cent of the off-licence wine market in Britain. The French are approaching 30 per cent – although in reality they are moving away from it because their percentage of the take-home wine market has been shrinking steadily for several years now. New Zealand's, it seems to me, can only burgeon, especially since there has been an increase in vineyards from 15,250 acres in 1993 to 18,750 acres in 1995. New Zealand may be a mere solo tympanist behind the massed strings of France, the percussive ranks of Italy or the huge brass section of Spain, yet its wines are always to be heard, fruity and distinctive, in spite of the overwhelming din from the rest of the players.

The French may explode morally repugnant atomic bombs in oceans which wash up on New Zealand's shores but the New Zealanders will have the last laugh. Their Sauvignons, when first they burst on the world scene just ten years ago in the shape of the incomparable Cloudy Bay, put a bomb under the French equivalents which is still going off and from the effects of which the Loire Sauvignon growers have never quite recovered.

ENGLAND'S FIRST WINE – MADE BY EARTHWORMS: THREE CHOIRS NEW RELEASE versus ALSACE RIESLING

Danie de Wet eased his bulk into the sofa in my sitting room and clasped his massive ursine hands together. He regarded the half-dozen bottles on the coffee table in front of him. He was oblivious to the curvaceous late afternoon London clouds of russet gold bobbing past the window. He looked grim. His wife, Leska, smiled, trying to be brave.

'The thing is… we've, er, never actually tried an English wine before,' she admitted.

But try all manner of other white wines the de Wets undoubtedly had. For Danie and Leska make delightful Chardonnays on their farm in Robertson in South Africa and so they also make it their business to taste all manner of other bottles from everywhere in the world.

'Well,' I said encouragingly to Leska in response to her remark, 'think of it like a memorable visit to the dentist. The experience will make a fascinating anecdote.'

But first, before we got to the bottle of five-year-old Three Choirs New Release white wine from the eponymous vineyard in Gloucestershire, we were going to enjoy some Alsatian wine, including a rare seven-year-old from a single *grand cru* vineyard, a Riesling from the legendary Hengst site.

Well, you know the end of this story, of course. The one wine we all wanted to stick with, the one wine we all wanted to finish before we went off to a local restaurant for dinner, was the Three Choirs. It was lean and clean, elegant, subtly fruity with a mineral undertone, and it tasted more concentrated and more purposefully delicious than any of the Alsatians.

'What's the grape here, Malcolm?' asked Danie.

I told him I wasn't sure. Was it Reichensteiner along with some other variety, like Seyval Blanc? Or was it a marriage of Huxelrebe and Madeleine Angevin? Danie looked mystified as I reeled off the names of these great varieties of England (all of which arrived via the grape laboratories of France and Germany). I might as well have recited a list of minor eleventh-century saints for all the sense a South African Chardonnay grower could make of them.

What I could say with assurance was that the wine was released for sale each year at the time in mid-November that the horrendous *beaujolais nouveau* appears in the shops. Not many bottles are produced – around 36,000 – and it costs just under £4 at various establishments, the best-known of which is the Co-op (and in some years, Victoria Wine). It is the first English wine released for sale after the same year's harvest.

But the curious thing is that in spite of being a wine which you would imagine would be drunk young – indeed, it is designed to be all gone by Christmas – I think it improves hugely with keeping for several years. It exhibits a big deposit of ice diamonds when you examine a five-year-old bottle, but rather than being harmful these are a positive benefit to the wine. Visible to the naked eye in the bottle, if the wine has been chilled, the presence of these crystals has aided the development of flavour and style. They are in fact tartrate crystals, a by-product of the fermentation process in which tartaric acid from the grape juice plays a significant role. In red wines such crystals appear as sediment and colour the cork deep scarlet, but in white wines like Three Choirs they look like a souvenir of a badly shattered windscreen. Yet not only are they not harmful, they tell the sensitive drinker that a conscientious and careful wine-maker has been at work who has not, as many supermarkets and wine retailers often demand, removed the crystals before bottling. This vandalism is perpetrated using various methods, but the easiest is simply to let the wine get so cold it almost freezes, when the crystals can be filtered out. Is this a good thing for wine? You bet it isn't. So next time you see crystals in a bottle of wine, don't complain, rejoice.

What have earthworms got to do with this? I was just coming to that.

A few years ago I paid a visit to Three Choirs vineyard, which from its beginnings as an apple orchard has branched into wine and become one of those eighties' enterprises based on the Business Expansion Scheme. A dozen shareholders came up with £40,000 each to develop the business as a commercial vineyard. Viticulturalist Tom Day, ex-merchant navy sailor and apple expert, was the man who ran the vineyard then, and he was as full of commitment to his vines as an uxorious groom to his bride. He was especially eloquent on the nature of the soil these vines were nourished in and the considerate treatment it received. For Tom was quick to remind me that what is used to treat the vines (under threat from disease and pests as a matter of course in a climate like England's), finds its way into the soil.

'We don't use insecticide. We employ some liquid seaweed. Wettable sulphur is the only fungicide. Copper? Yes, we use some copper spray. But,' and here the ebullient Mr Day paused and threw back his shoulders, and his bearded jowls set themselves seriously before he smiled and looked exactly like sleuth/restaurateur Henry Crabbe on Sunday night BBC TV, 'you must never use copper to excess ... it'll interfere with the earthworms.'

'Ah!' I muttered knowingly.

'We have a very viable earthworm population in the vineyard here. They aerate the red sandstone soil the vine roots depend on and keep it healthy. Earthworms are my partners in producing good grapes.'

> ❝ It was enough for one evening that they had discovered that English wine can be delicious. ❞

Uncertain as to how South Africans, especially a couple hungry for their dinner, regarded such creatures, I spared the de Wets the intimate details of this relationship. It was enough for one evening that they had discovered that English wine can be delicious.

Mondavi Reserve Cabernet 1991 (California, USA) versus Chateau Latour 1991 (Bordeaux, France)

Mr Mondavi is the stuff of legend; a sort of Gary Cooper figure as that actor appeared in *High Noon*, having a seemingly unique and individual reputation for standing alone against all the odds. But it wasn't Mr Robert Mondavi I met once I had negotiated the bulldozers in the Mondavi winery car park (busy reconstructing the winery landscape to turn the place into a sort of Disneyland for wine lovers) but Mr Michael Mondavi, along with a colleague of his, a young fellow who worked in public relations and who coolly mentioned that he had a little winery of his own on the side.

Now, no one can say that this company isn't interested in exporting. Indeed, with sales growth in this area of around 25 per cent annually they are certainly the most dynamic exporter of high-quality wine in California. True, I didn't go a bundle on the Blush wine I was offered, a white Zinfandel made by allowing the red grapes only the minimum skin contact with the juice, but the **Napa Cabernet Sauvignon Reserves** I tasted were largely superb – one of them, the '91, easily outfruiting a **Chateau Latour** from France of the same year which my hosts insisted on opening in order to demonstrate their own comfortable superiority.

I protested at the opening of this 100-dollar bottle of imported chateau-bottled Bordeaux. Comparisons are odorous, even odious. This is well known. Besides, I pleaded, I was the last wine writer on earth who required further proof of how rich and soft and ready to drink a great Californian Cabernet can be in contrast to a withdrawn, stuffy, up-its-own-fundament claret of massively overwrought reputation and absurd price.

My entreaties fell on a deaf set of ears. A performance was being put on for me and the play must run its course. The ending was just as I had anticipated.

2 | BLISS! END-OF-THE-WORKDAY SOLVENTS

'…we went on to discuss wines, whiskies, and Worthington's., and I rounded it up… "Ah! yes, it's only when the day is over that the day really begins – what?"
W.N.P. Barbellion,
Journal of a Disappointed Man, 1948

M any alcoholic drinks are effective solvents. That is to say, pleasing early evening liquids wash off the mental grime of the day and restore us to our clean, sparkling shiniest. Wine is perfect in this role. There is, however, a deal of difference between wine which is chosen to accompany a certain food and one picked to go with a particular mood. The latter is either sipped for pleasure or drunk as an aperitif, with or without tidbits to hand. But either way, at the end of the day, scorning the pub, we can retire to our own nook and, as the front door closes behind us and the wickedness of public transport or the motorway and the sheer bloodymindedness of humanity in general (as personally experienced over the past eight hours) is shut out, open what we damn well please.

I am a great fan of wine boxes (more details in Chapter 12) in these circumstances, especially if you are contemplating dinner with further wine out later, or you simply don't want to drink more than a single glass. And a single glass will do to rinse away the blues of the day and put a glow in your cheeks or fresh resolve in your heart. A wine like **Stowells Chilean Sauvignon Blanc** (around £13 the 3-litre box at Waitrose, Morrison and Victoria Wine Cellars) is a perfectly

> **6** And a single glass will do to rinse away the blues of the day and put a glow in your cheeks or fresh resolve in your heart. **9**

delicious, dry, fruity white which is economic (45p a glass) and stays fresh, once the tap has been turned, for five weeks.

A wine which is an end-of-the-workday solvent is usually fresh and young, red or white depending upon choice. It could be rosé during the summer months, but outstanding examples of this style of wine at a reasonable price are rare. My two favourites, and I have literally only two, are **Hungarian Cabernet Sauvignon Nagyrede Rosé** at Safeway and Sainsbury, and **Santa Helena Chilean Rosé** at Asda. Expect to pay between £3 and £4.

I've also chosen to include in this chapter a few of the revealing wine trips I've embarked upon, because the wines involved are all early evening tipples. Not every solvent wine, it should be noted, must of necessity be inexpensive. Generally, they tend to be so, but there are times, as with certain examples below, when you want to reward yourself with something of a delicate yet incisive complexity which is highly individual and special – when, say, you have been trampled over by a workday of uncommon cruelty and vindictiveness but emerged triumphant.

Certain well-established wines which have been traditional solvents are nowadays overrated and overpriced yet still sell well to those drinkers possessing cement-mixers for palates and pockets of great depth but scant discrimination. I recommend we should scourge these poor wines and suggest we go for more modern, fruitier, better-balanced alternatives. Thus Sancerre (£7–£9) gets the elbow but **Chilean Sauvignon Blanc** (widely available up to £3.99), southern French beauties like **Domaine St Marc Sauvignon Blanc Vin de Pays d'Oc** (Sainsbury, £3.75), and **Vredendal Sauvignon Blanc** (Safeway, £3.49) are all heartily recommended. Beaujolais is abominable – never touch it unless a bribe of National Lottery proportions is being offered you. But if you do find this an irresistible inducement, I forgive this violation of your principles on the understanding that you will stand me a case of a) Kekfrancos from Hungary;

b) Merlot from Bulgaria; or c) Pinotage from South Africa. All these examples of fresh, fruity redness take deliciously to a light chilling and are delightful companions at the end of the day. Over the past couple of years the tastiest examples of these wines that I have drunk are as follows:

▶ **Hungarian Country Red wines (all under £3.50)**
Asda's Hungarian Cabernet Sauvignon 1993
Asda's Hungarian Merlot 1993
Hungaroo Merlot 1992 (Co-op)
Great Plain Kekfrancos 1993 (Safeway)
Hungarian Country Wine, Kiskoros Region 1993 (Safeway)
Private Reserve Cabernet Sauvignon, Villany 1993 (Safeway)
Tesco's Reka Valley Hungarian Merlot
Villany Hills Cabernet Sauvignon 1992 (Thresher)
Cabernet Sauvignon, Szekszard NV (Victoria Wine)
Villany Cabernet Sauvignon, Szekszard 1993 (Victoria Wine)
Sopron Cabernet Sauvignon 1994 (Waitrose)

▶ **Bulgarian Merlot (all under a fiver)**
Cabernet Merlot 1993 (Booths)
Vintage Premier Merlot, Iambol Region 1994 (Thresher)
Bulgarian Merlot/Gamay, Russe 1993 (Spar)
Reserve Merlot, Lovico Suhindol 1991 (Sainsbury)
Vintage Blend Oriachovitza Merlot & Cabernet Sauvignon Reserve 1990 (Sainsbury)
Sainsbury's Oak Aged Bulgarian Merlot, Liubimetz Region 1993
Bulgarian Country Wine (Merlot/Pinot Noir), Sliven (Victoria Wine)
Merlot/Cabernet Sauvignon, Liubimetz 1994 (Kwik Save)
Safeway's Young Vatted Merlot, Rousse 1994
Oriachovitza Barrel-aged Merlot 1994 (Waitrose)
Stambolovo Merlot Reserve 1990 (Somerfield)

▶ **South African Pinotage (all under six quid)**
Cape Afrika Pinotage *(Co-op)*
Fair Cape Pinotage 1992 *(Morrison)*
Beyerskloof Pinotage 1991 *(Oddbins)*
Kleindal Pinotage 1995 *(Safeway)*
Simonsvlei Pinotage/Cabernet Reserve 1994 *(Safeway)*
Fairview Pinotage, Paarl 1995 *(Sainsbury)*
Sainsbury's South African Pinotage
Tesco's Beyers Truter Pinotage
Avontuur Pinotage, Stellenbosch 1995 *(Waitrose)*
Clos Malverne Pinotage Reserve, Stellenbosch 1994 *(Waitrose)*
Diamond Hills Pinotage/Cabernet Sauvignon 1994 *(Waitrose)*

GREAT END-OF-THE-WORKDAY SOLVENTS: DANIE DE WET'S CHARDONNAYS FROM THE DE WETSHOF ESTATE, ROBERTSON, SOUTH AFRICA. (FROM TESCO'S OWN-LABEL AT £3.99 TO VARIOUS DIFFERENT BLENDS OF CHARDONNAY AT WINE SHOPS AND SUPERMARKETS FROM £4.99 TO £7.99)

The truly phenomenal **Danie De Wet Grey Label Chardonnay 1993** at £4.99 was a pedigree bargain. Danie makes many different Chardonnays but this Grey Label of his was mind-stretching and the very opposite of grey. It was profusely fruity without being overrich, had lovely woody delicacy and a delicious citrus finish. It stuck in my mind long after I drank it, and you might still find the odd bottle in regional wine merchants who've been a bit slow to sell it through. A touch classy for an end-of-the-workday solvent? Well, not when you've had a great workday. Then, a penn'orth short of a fiver is not a lot to pay for a superbly soothing white wine of such patent style and quality that it gives you plenty to chew on, such are its complexity and thought-provoking structure, without the need for any food to accompany it. But in contrast to the delicacy of the wine stands the remarkable man who makes it.

Danie de Wet is a big person; his hospitality is big, his handshake is colossal, his grin, delivered two metres up, radiates warmth, and the vines on his farm on the Breede River in Robertson stretch for 350 acres. Danie is a man who is steeped in tradition yet uses the latest technology to specialize in one great grape variety, Chardonnay (well, almost one – he sneaked me a preview of a Riesling he's experimenting with when I encountered him at the London Wine Fair last). On his farm, he has used for years the ingenious computer-controlled irrigation equipment developed in Israel and which brought flowers to the deserts of that country. Danie also uses technology in the winery – stainless-steel tanks and computers and so on – yet it is his own delicate handling of grape juice allied to his immense skills at blending all the various tanks and barrels of his Chardonnays which make him one of the world's masters of the grape.

▶ **Danie's various wines and retailers**

Danie de Wet Chardonnay 1995 *(Oddbins)*

De Wetshof Chardonnay d'Honneur *(Oddbins and Thresher)*

Danie de Wet Chardonnay sur Lie 1995 *(Safeway)*

Danie de Wet Grey Label Chardonnay 1994 *(Sainsbury)*

Danie de Wet Green Label Chardonnay 1994 *(Tesco)*

Danie de Wet De Lesca Chardonnay 1995 *(Thresher and Victoria Wine)*

A WINE JOURNALIST'S REVENGE ON HIS READERS. (AND HOW HE DISCOVERED ROMANIAN PINOT NOIR – FROM SAINSBURY'S NON-VINTAGE BLEND AT £2.99 TO MORRISON'S WONDROUS 1990 RESERVE AT £3.29 – AND WHAT OCCURRED WHEN HE WENT IN SEARCH OF IT)

Romania has always had great potential. That is why the ambitious Romans wanted it so badly that many of them died to possess it. Yet even though anyone who speaks Italian will get by without difficulty in Romania, some of the original Dacian lives on in some 2000 words in current use which derive from that ancient tongue.

Psychologically, the wines speak no Italian at all. Their tongue is French. I mean by this that it is French viticultural and oenological methods which have dominated the ideas of Romanian grape-growers and wine-makers for decades. But this is, I am pleased to report, the old-style approach which vanished from much of the French wine scene in the early 1960s. Since the revolution in Romania, modern wine-making ideas are being adopted to enhance, rather than sup-plant, the traditional methods.

Romanian Pinot Noir is sold all over the shop. Examples abound at all the supermarkets and most of the high street wine shops, and while many make terrific end-of-the-work-day solvents, some are grander and more complex (yet are not a lot more expensive).

The first retailer to ship in a great one was J Sainsbury. Indeed, via the rich fruit and classy structure of Romanian Pinot Noir I gained revenge on all those *Guardian* readers who wrote to me, some years ago now, complaining bitterly at my recommendation of Chilean Sauvignon Blanc and Cabernet Sauvignon. At the time Chile was only just emerg-ing from the wicked constrictions of the Pinochet regime, a political situation I must confess I found sufficiently repug-nant to disbar me from writing about the country's wines, but at the appropriate moment (a plebiscite restoring democracy) I decided it was now time to check the wines out and see if they were good enough to recommend. I drank one brilliant bottle after another. But several readers of my Superplonk column, when Chilean wines duly appeared in print, still found them impossible to stomach and ticked me off in no uncertain terms. I read the letters and licked my wounds.

A little over a month later the magic philtre fell into my hands. If Chile had one of the most egregious scoundrels since the Second World War running the show, then surely Romania had one of the worst of the century. But the revelations about Mr and Mrs Ceaucescu's evils were only just beginning to seep out into the Western press and the full horror story was some weeks away from its final, sudden, devastating chapter. It was at this time that a bottle of Romanian Pinot Noir, a non-vintage wine to be going on sale at Sainsbury, fell into my hands.

It was superb. It had the true varietal character of the Pinot Noir, a delicious rich, gamy, almost heady quality allied to a deep cherry and wild raspberry fruit, and it was supremely delicious and sinfully drinkable. It was also mature, having been raised in oak barrels for some years, and so it was astonishing value at around £2.50 a bottle. I rated it highly and said so at the earliest opportunity.

The Saturday *Guardian* starts thumping on readers' doormats around 7.30 a.m., I suppose. Sainsbury doesn't open the doors of any of its hundreds of stores until a little while later. However, by 10.45 that morning, so a man from the store's head office told me later, there was barely a bottle of Romanian Pinot Noir left standing on any Sainsbury shelf in the land. *Guardian* readers had thrown themselves into their Volvo estates and plundered nigh on every bottle. And I received not one word of criticism from any reader. Even when the month was out, and Ceaucescu had been fully unmasked as the vilest of the vile, every bottle had vanished and still not a single admonitory syllable reached my ears or was carried up my front path by my postwoman. (I did have a postwoman at the time who wore trousers, but she was replaced by a chap called Pat, would you believe, who wore a pigtail.)

In a subsequent column I was able to point out the hypocritical irony of this situation. I have never since received a letter about Chile – although certain diehards disliked me writing about South Africa despite Mr Mandela's release – and I got some comments about French wine when the French underground nuclear testing programme commenced. But on the political implications of buying Pinot Noir from Romania, readers have restricted their disgruntlement to complaints that they couldn't get their hands on enough of it. As you can imagine, therefore, I experienced a mixture of feelings when I toured Romania – the Ceaucescus dead and buried – and visited the winery which turned out this remarkable wine. When I finally reached Dealul Mare, the area from where some of the richest Romanian Pinot Noir comes, it was not a vineyard or a winery my hosts were anxious for me to see, but the National Research Institute for Vine and Wine. And here all that stood out initially were the cigars. For a moment I wondered if the other men in the room, short-sleeve-shirted and pungently cherooted, would produce a pack of cards and begin a poker school. But the director of the Institute arrived and the holiday atmosphere ceased. Employing a fully extended car radio aerial, the director jabbed at a map of the country. I moved discreetly to the back of the room, unable to breathe or see my notebook in the fug. The radio aerial ranged over the vinous map of Romania, the green bits receiving emphatic whacks.

I held my hand up. 'Can I please see the vineyard and the winery and meet the man who makes the Pinot Noir – please?'

'You mean, Mr Gluck, you aren't interested in lectures and statistics and learning valuable information?'

And then it dawned on me. All those decades under communist autocracy had bred a suspicion of individual achievement. That Pinot Noir was lauded as a team effort. To be sure, I finally got to see the vineyard and the winery – nothing new at either place – but the man who actually laid claim to making the wine, and there must be a wine-maker at the bottom of it somewhere, was never even named. I was forced to settle for this and we moved on.

Later, accompanied by a gypsy accordionist and a bead-skirted singer, I had my lunch. Romania has a rumbustiously

Rabelaisian approach to table, at least when it entertains wine writers, and five courses are just a trifling snack. I limited myself to a dozen radishes and three dozen raw spring garlics for my first course. Should Count Dracula fancy English blood on the drive through Transylvania and the Carpathians, planned for later that day, I felt I should be suitably repugnant. The luncheon wine was wonderful – more Pinot Noir. It went well with the stomach soup with raw chillies floating in it.

EARLY DAYS IN A NEW REPUBLIC: MORAVIA – FEATURING (IN A SMALL WALK-ON PART) MORAVIAN VINEYARD SPECIAL CUVÉE PINOT GRIS 1994

'*So what happens if a bird foraging in a conventional vineyard eats a worm and then craps as it is flying over an organic vineyard? The organic vineyard loses its status?*'

'*I'm sorry. I cannot translate that.*'

(Conversation between wine writer and local schoolteacher acting as interpreter)

The old Czechoslovakia was physically breaking up into separate republics as I drove across the border from Hungary. I was reminded of a child bored with his Lego, pulling it apart. Once past the urban sprawl of Brno I nearly ran over a border guard who was haphazardly positioning a barrier across the motorway. I was permitted to pass without demur, to end up eating Wiener schnitzels in the Gambrinus Weinstube in the town of Velke Bilovice. I had a disjointed conversation with a middle-aged Moravian who for some reason never satisfactorily explained supported Southampton Football Club. However, his recommendation of which Czech beer to drink was fully grasped and his advice, followed to the letter, led to a refreshingly light yet hoppy lager.

Breakfast next morning at the Hotel Zerotin consisted of scrambled egg and sausages and I was interested to note that two truck drivers at the opposite table washed theirs down with giant tankards of the same beer I had drunk last night. How did the Russian military ever cower a people like this? Bruce Chatwin supplies the answer (via his novel *Utz*, which is about a porcelain collector in Prague): 'The Czechs' propensity to "bend" before superior forces was not necessarily a weakness. Rather, their metaphysical view of life encouraged them to look on acts of force as ephemera.' I popped egg and sausage into my mouth and thought how Buddhist this made the Czechs seem, though the beefy truckers opposite seemed unlikely members of any pacific religious sect.

The next Czech I met (or was he now a Moravian?) was Jan Kaspar, sales director of the Vinium winery in Velke Pavlovice, just up the road from Velke Bilovice. It is from here that Safeway, with the oenological assistance of Australians Nick Butler and Mark Nairn who make the wine at Vinium, bought the uncommonly toothsome **Moravian Vineyard Pinot Gris 1994** (which is white, superbly apricot-edged yet fresh and invigorating, varietally faithful, and stunningly stylish for the money).

Mr Kaspar was once a trainee at Marks and Spencer and he appears young enough, and sufficiently smartly turned out, to be still so employed. There is an interesting painting on the Vinium board-room wall depicting seventeenth-century drunks abusing themselves in a filthy cellar. I feel cheered by this. The wines I tasted abused no one, except for a sparkler of bruising acidity which ricocheted off the roof of my mouth like gunshot. The striking woman, dark and glowering like a barely extinguished fire, who poured out these wines was patently related to the youngest man in the painting.

The other winery I saw that day, before I crossed the border into the land of my Austrian grandfathers, was in the historic town of Valtice. The town itself, like a film set for a comic opera, is dominated by the mansion of the long-gone Liechtenstein family. It is said that Roman soldiers first planted vines here in the third century AD, although I always find myself falling asleep when some worthy refers to Romans being the first to make wine in a particular area. How much more interesting to be told that this was the first town in the Austro-Hungarian empire to own up to a licensed prostitute and — look! — there is the apartment above the butcher's shop where she plied her trade during the course of which she passed on syphilis to the homosexual Crown Prince Rupprecht's bisexual ostler and changed the whole course of Middle European history! Alas, none of this is true. But you can see why the romantic, who might contrive a deeply compelling story about such a person, often makes a more engaging companion than the factualist, who can be inclined to dryness. You may need reminding that Marcus Probus occupied the Imperial throne at the time. Marcus is famous for being famous for absolutely nothing — including the inauguration of vineyards.

Certainly the wines are nothing to make a fuss about, even though the town boasts the only college of viticulture in the Czech Republic, and the Viennese flood across the border in their Mercedes and BMWs to trough and swig at the Liechtenstein palace, now a hotel and restaurant, where the prices are a meagre fraction of Austria's. Its engine compartment stove in two by the impact, a car lies sprawled across the entrance to this hotel, a lamp-post where the fascia panel once lay. A permanent memorial to automania, so I was told. To which the only intelligent response is that surely the sight of it causes more accidents than it prevents; indeed, as we gawp at this wreck several tourists stop their cars, jam the road, and snap away with their cameras.

Valtice winery? Well now, here's a thing. Organic wines

come from here, and the organic vineyards they are grown in lie very near to inorganic vineyards. Hence my question about birds and worms. I tasted some of these organic wines and I quote from my notes: '…these have little aroma and less fruit and their freshness is more a result of the absence of these two characteristics than a positive aspect of their structure'.

But what of Safeway's magnificent bargain, the **Special Cuvee Pinot Gris?** The bad news is that the '94 is all gone and the '95 vintage was all mixed with Traminer, another grape variety, to make a blend before Safeway could get its hands on it. But the 1996 vintage is being anticipated with some excitement. The wine takes a year in bottle to develop its brilliant character and so we have some time to wait. But, fingers crossed, from spring 1997 the new wine should be on sale. It will, I hope, be a classic end-of-the-workday solvent.

GREAT END-OF-THE WORKDAY SOLVENT (NO. 2): GRGICH HILLS CHARDONNAY – A LITTLE PIECE OF CROATIA IN CALIFORNIA

Mike Grgich, one half of Grgich Hills Cellar, looks like ex-President Mitterrand, the late wily old fox of France. And he dresses like the ex-President – an ex-President off-duty and relaxed, enjoying a Sunday in the country with his grand-children. The face has rivulets of warm feeling which run through it like dry riverbeds in some hospitable southern region. The shirt is plaid, buttoned up to the collar and tie-less. On Mr Grgich's head is a beret, generous as a ten-person pan-cake in size but dark blue in colour and with the customary stalk in the middle. Yet a name like Grgich; … pronouncing it makes you feel like a Rottweiler warming up its throat.

'I was born in Croatia. I graduated in wine science from the university at Zagreb. And nine years of communism was enough for me, so I jumped out, went through West Germany, Canada and came here to California in 1958. I worked twenty years for other wineries where I made all the mistakes somebody else was paying for, so now that I've opened my own winery I'm not supposed to make mistakes. But I was very lucky to work with Beaulieu Vineyards which used to be the number one winery in all of California in those days under Andre Tchelistcheff. And then I worked with Robert Mondavi for four years and then Chateau Montalena. It was at Montalena that the Chardonnay which I made in 1973 was tasted at a Paris wine competition, by nine French judges, and my wine was in first place. I was born again! Can you imagine: *Time* Magazine called me from New York? I said, my goodness, what's wrong, do they want to put me in jail? They wanted to interview me. So since then I really got proud and became convinced I could make good wine. Many wineries wanted to hire me as a wine-maker. But I didn't want that. I wanted to go on my own. However I didn't have money and I didn't have a vineyard. Then I met Mr Hills, who wanted me to make wine for him from his vineyard, and we came together as partners and started Grgich Hills.'

Mr Grgich – Mike – is telling me this sitting one side of a wooden picnic table, me the other, which is standing on a patio outside his winery. It is early morning but the sun is already high enough to cause the trees to throw dappled shadows on the tiles at our feet. Did I say early morning? Not so early that I haven't already sipped a few of the Grgich Hills wines: an '87 Chardonnay (delicate, citrussy), a '91 Chardonnay (still developing), a '92 Fumé Blanc (full and fruity), an '89 Cabernet Sauvignon (solid, rounded, flavoursome), an '83 Cabernet Sauvignon (fruit beginning to show its age), and a Zinfandel. This Zinfandel

was of the 1989 vintage and it had, in an international wine competition in 1994, been voted the best Zinfandel in the world. I found it restrained and delicate, certainly impressive, good bouquet, firm, spicy fruit, but still young and improving. I felt that its complexity would not arrive in real depth for another five years because the tannins were still shrouding the fruit somewhat. But… but at least I'd realized a dream! I drank my first ever Zinfandel in the sunshine of its birthplace: California. But listen. Mr Grgich is speaking.

'Grgich Hills has made consistency and longevity the hallmark of its wines, our wines. This is not a typical thing for the United States. Americans they change every year the shape of their things: like cars … change, change, change. I maybe changed something in our wines but I kept the same style. So when people drink my wine in 1980 and they try my wine in 1990, it's not much different, just better.'

This is a man with a deeply philosophical turn of mind. But I'm not given much chance to ponder on this for he's in full flow.

'The same style. Yes! Our wine at Grgich Hills has a longevity that no other wine in America has. American white wines when I came to California used to be good for six months on the shelf and then they'd oxidate. Last year, the wine inspector tasted a lot of the Chardonnays which I made between 1972 and 1992 – twenty vintages! In the whole world I have never heard of twenty vintages of a white wine tasted vertically. And all of them scored good. The '73 Chardonnay at the Paris competition tasting in 1993 – that is twenty years later – scored 95 out of 100.'

> **❝ Every winery survives in its own way and my way is to see to it that I have consistency. ❞**

I was itching to maybe get invited to taste this wine. But with a scratch of his ear Mr Grgich was developing his ideas further.

'So we have consistency and longevity. Every winery survives in its own way and my way is to see to it that I have consistency. Some people change their label every year. My labels are the same as long as I live. So our style and our philosophy are consistency. Through this we have discovered that we have longevity.'

He felt satisfied now that he'd explained himself fully. However, there is an aspect of this man's approach to the fermentation process which allows the wines he makes to age in the way that they do. This approach concerns the secondary fermentation stage, through which all wine will pass if permitted. This second stage is called malolactic fermentation.

There are, you see, two ferments with wine. The first is the alcoholic fermentation. The crucial component here is the yeasts which are either present on the skins of the grapes or are introduced into the wine by the wine-maker so that he or she has more control over the style of the wine. This latter process is called yeast inoculation. Various types of yeast are available commercially and each will contribute to making a different style of wine; indeed, some wine-makers make different batches of wine from the same grape variety but using different sorts of yeast and then they blend the resultingly different wines into one bottled product. But this is not common practice. Having found a yeast type he or she likes, the wine-maker will stick with it and exercise firm control over the finished product.

The yeast does a supremely simple job. It gobbles up the sugar in the grapes and transforms it into alcohol. A wine may be allowed to finish its ferment or it may be stopped. It depends on the degree of alcohol required. Alcohol, as it rises in strength during a ferment, will finally kill off the yeast at around 15.2 per cent. But how many wines reach it? Very few (thank goodness). With some wines, like, say, certain Germans, the level of sugar in the grapes is only sufficient to reach a certain degree of alcoholic strength which may be quite low. But the style required in the wine determines the final alcohol level. Thus a bone-dry wine has little sugar left in it because the ferment was allowed to go as far as it could before stopping naturally, or the ferment may have been stopped by the wine-maker and some residual sugar left in to add weight to the fruitiness in the wine. In certain sweet wines, like dessert styles, the grapes will be picked deliberately overripe and bursting with sugar and so when the ferment stops, or is stopped, there will still be plenty of sugar left unconverted into alcohol. Unfermented grape juice, which is sweet, is often added to a finished wine to give it fruitiness in a year when the grapes were low in sugar, or sugar may be added during the ferment to raise the alcohol level beyond that which the grapes could attain naturally. It all depends on the style of wine required by the wine-maker.

> **The yeast does a supremely simple job. It gobbles up the sugar in the grapes and transforms it into alcohol.**

However, more mysterious than the widely understood and appreciated chemical phenomenon of the alcoholic fermentation is the secondary fermentation in which the malic acid present in the new wine goes through a totally natural transformation into lactic acid. This transformation, broadly, means that the malic acid, which is sharp and apple-like, is converted into the softer lactic, or milk-like, acid. Most red wines go through this secondary fermentation stage as a matter of course, though not all: beaujolais, for instance, owes some of its freshness to its malic acidity, and in other young, fresh reds the degree of malolactic transformation may have been only partially permitted. However, a high degree of malolactic ferment, the full 100 per cent, would be customary with a red wine where softness is required to dominate over crispness, as in wines from Bordeaux or Rioja or many other places.

Now, like the inoculation with artificial yeasts to get the primary ferment going, the secondary ferment can also be controlled by induction. Bacteria are required for this, especially in circumstances where none is in natural residence in the winery or lurking in the barrels which may be used for storing and mel

lowing the wine. Thus the appropriate bacteria may be introduced before the alcoholic ferment is finished, for it is quite possible for both ferments to coincide, although, as you might expect, the secondary one rarely, if ever, begins before the primary has got going. In Mr Grgich's winery, secondary fermentation for his Chardonnays is frowned upon. Let him explain, in response to a question of mine.

"Now, sir,' I started. 'Tell me about the chemical key which permits your Chardonnays to enjoy such longevity. Tell me about your Chardonnays and the way you deny them the opportunity to undergo secondary fermentation. How do you inhibit the malolactic?'

Mr Grgich nodded keenly at this question, glad to have been given a chance to expound his ideas further.

'To tell you the short story of how I stopped malolactic fermentation or how I ensure it doesn't happen is this: I have experience of how to do it. And it's easy if you have experience and you know how. I started handling malolactic fermentation in 1960. I first established a system how to induce malolactic fermentation. So I know much more about it because I did lots of experimentation: how to start it and the opposite of this, which is prohibiting. I learned that the malolactic will be enhanced if you stir up the must, if you have lower sucrose, if you have a warmer temperature, and if you have bacteria. The more bacteria you have, the faster it goes. So I did the opposite. Any bacteria in my wine I sterilized – so there was no chance to get any bacteria. Our barrels are sterile – we put in brand new barrels which had never had malolactic fermentation. I keep those barrels for use only with Sauvignon Blanc and Chardonnay. And I have no problems. Many people have problems. They cannot stop the malolactic fermentation. I never had one barrel in this winery in seventeen years that did go to malolactic fermentation, because it can't. I wanted to prevent it and I did. Not many people have the experience, or did the experimentation with malolactic that I did. Mainly the wineries here have somebody in a laboratory, a microbiologist or somebody, and the wine-maker doesn't know anything about microbiology, he's just a wine-maker.

'I used to be everything. I used to be chemist, microbiologist, and wine-maker, and salesman! In one person! The connection gets lost through many people, but I was very fortunate that when I started at Beaulieu Vineyards it was as Quality Controller. I was the first Quality Controller in any Napa Valley winery. So I knew the systems of quality control. As well as watching the grapes in the vineyard, my job was to watch fermentation. My job was everywhere: when they racked the wine, filtered the wine, fined the wine, bottled the wine. I had all this under my control. And I was widely educated, but many people have one person on different sections and they never connect and what one has experienced the other hasn't so they cannot harmonize. I carried on another five years and then I became wine-maker.'

'Such wines must be raw in their youth,' I observed.

'But you see, my Chardonnay doesn't go on the market until it's five years old. It sits here for five years in this winery and harmonizes, improves. And my wine definitely improves through this.'

'It's a pity drinkers in Britain don't get more chance to enjoy your Chardonnays,' I said, wondering how such wines would go down with a market fond of the buttery richness to be found in so many New World Chardonnays. It is this butteriness which tells the nose, and the palate, of the investigative drinker that a measure of malolactic fermentation has taken place. This is because a substance called diacetyl is produced during the malolactic stage and this both smells and tastes of butter. It is an attractive feature of many Australian Chardonnays nowadays, but not so many years ago the amount of diacetyl in Oz whites was so great and mouthfilling that a mere glass of such wine was enough for me – even with rich food. But over the past five years, it seems to me the Aussies' control of *le malo* (as the French call the secondary ferment) has become firmer and less exuberantly expressive, and better-balanced white wines are the result.

'I don't know about exporting,' said Mr Grgich. 'I'm as much business-oriented as I am a wine-maker. If I sell here at the winery I get most financially out of it. People pay and carry. I don't have to bill them. I have no unpaid bills. When I go into export, though we have fax and telephone, it's not easy to connect. Everywhere people are trying to give discounts to exports. That means if we sell to England, we get less money than if we sell in California. So financially we have no incentive. I can sell everything I produce in the State I live in. Mr Hills, my partner, used to travel in England. He met Mr Pope and they wanted to have a few Californian wines, and so we started with him maybe selling a hundred cases a year ... '

What chance do we ordinary mortals stand if the Pope can only get that few wines out of you? I thought. The Pope could be any one of four extant eponyms running the Dorset wine merchant Eldridge Pope and Co (a plc no less) which, in the teeth of Mr Grgich's indifference to exports, regularly acquires Grgich Hills wines for sale to the public at large.

'In the old days,' Mr Grgich continued, 'people said all roads lead to Rome. Now it is London. Definitely publicity lives in London. England is very important. For wine, London is still the centre of the world.'

And then he scratched his ear and looked off into the

> **❝ For wine, London is still the centre of the world. ❞**

distance. 'Even if we're short of wine we would be able to give more to England if they're interested,' he added reflectively.

I wondered aloud if his labels weren't a bit plain for the English market. There was nothing on the back, as with most Aussie bottles for example, to tempt the customer with an exotic tale of derring-do.

'I'm one of the old-timers. In the old country, they would say that if a woman she opens up everything in her heart to you, you won't try to discover anything. So we have a very simple label. As little information as possible. So people have to discover. They have to dig in the bottle and discover what's in the bottle. I would like people to judge wine by the wine inside – not by stories. I was surprised when I first came to America and the man running this winery I was working at he told me how he created stories because customers wanted stories. People asked him: how did you get the name for your wine? So he made up this story. In the old country I never needed that. When I came here I still had in my mind the European style. I don't see the necessity of stories.'

Stroll on, Mr Friendly Rottweiler. You began telling me a wonderful story the moment I sat down. And I've swallowed every word of it. If you care to experience the Grgich magic in similar throat-enchanting fashion, you may telephone one of the four Popes, all misters, at Eldridge Pope and Co on 01305 251251. Or you can visit their premises at Weymouth Avenue, Dorchester – a county town which is something of a story in itself since not only was it the Caer-Dori of the woad-encrusted ancients (and the Dunium of the Romans) but it was central to two of literature's greatest stories: Thomas Hardy's *The Mayor of Casterbridge* and John Cowper Powys's *Maiden Castle*. I can think of few pleasures more profound than to be sat in the sun with one or other of these two novels, a bottle of Grgich Hills Chardonnay within easy reach. Or, just as happy a contemplation, to have such treats waiting for me when I get home of an evening.

3 | BRITAIN'S FAVOURITE FOODS LOVE WINE

(HATE BEER)

I first fell in love with the idea of food and wine in the late May of 1964 when I was somewhat younger than I am today. Indeed, so young, raw, and unploughed was I that I considered a thirty-year-old woman to be an older woman. Nevertheless, I fell in love and I've never forgotten her. She was French (of course) and swathed from head to toe in light brown suède, until bedtime (of course) when she wore a skimpy negligée of frilly design which revealed more than it concealed – an aspect of woman's inhumanity to man I was as yet too fresh to fully appreciate. Yes, dear reader, this is a kiss-and-tell story.

But it was not the older French woman herself I embraced. It was her philosophy.

It was warm for May in Gaillac, a town in that part of France we British, unlike any local, refer to as the Dordogne. And I was, let me remind you, a native of that island race which the French regard as knowing everything about eating but next to nothing about food. It was my first trip abroad and it was to change my life, leading directly, twenty-four years later, to my embarking on the career path of wine scribbling.

The setting was a hotel in Gaillac's main square, just as the sun had gone down, and some hours behind the time my elder brother had informed the hotel we would arrive – this was the second stop on our drive from London to Spain to enjoy a family holiday in a house rented for the first two weeks in June. The hotel was not upset at our lateness; they seemed more concerned that the kitchen was closing and they would be unable to demonstrate the full range of the chef's extraordinary powers.

It is not our meal that is of interest here (though I can recall every magic moment of my first taste of wild mushrooms), but the meal, two-thirds finished, being relished by the suède-suited Frenchwoman and her male companion of equally advanced age at the adjacent table in the dining room. They were both slim but they ate like Trojans after a week without fodder: I was witness only to the vast cheeseboard they devoured, the second bottle of red wine, the dessert, and the goldfish bowls of Armagnac they thirstily swallowed. If this was the final flourish of their meal, how extravagant and wonderful had been the major part which I had missed? When they finished, they threw down their napkins and sighed. Would they be able to stand? I wondered. But stand they did. They wished us goodnight. "They'll sleep like babes," said my mother.

But no babe slept like they did, for when, an hour later, I staggered replete to bed, I discovered that my room was directly above theirs and this ancient French couple were standing on the balcony, arm-in-arm, dressed for bed, talking softly to the gibbous moon which glowed misshapenly down. I was utterly thunderstruck. How could romance blossom after such a feast? But he was sighing, she was cooing, and the pair of them were disgracefully underdressed. They jointly threw a kiss to the moon and went inside, leaving their door ajar. It was obvious that conversation was at an end and some other pursuit was on the menu.

A great secret of life was being revealed to me here and I have never forgotten it. It is a simple secret: always arrive late at small provincial French hotels. It offers the curious diner a more adventurous menu with the possibility of cabaret on the side.

Ever since that time, and most enthusiastically in the days in Spain which followed and the years in London afterwards, I was under the sway of the giddy concept of food and drink and female companionship (of all ages) and I have never recovered my balance. It was to cost me dear. I asked every likely, and unlikely, lass out to dinner, and quickly developed the trick of remembering which wines were good and which wines were bad in all the cheap restaurants, mainly Italian but some French, one Spanish and one Chinese (for Chinatown in Soho was not yet up and running), to which my passions led me. I also discovered a good deal about which wines went with what foods, and I have never stopped making discoveries.

The New World wines we British drinkers can avail ourselves of so reasonably are another of the most exciting of these discoveries of recent years and one reason why I admire such wines. Travelling to so many of the world's vineyards has also given me an insight into the food and wine pairings the wine-makers themselves enjoy and which are often a revelation to us in the UK (like very dry Fino sherry with prawns and ham dishes and South African red Pinotage with grilled fish). However, it is these New World wines which have opened up the diner's horizons so widely because so many of these wines are better suited to the kinds of foods we now enjoy in Britain. The wines of Chile, the Pacific states of the USA, South Africa, Australia and New Zealand, as well as the increasing number of New World-style wines from European areas like northern Spain, southern Italy and Eastern Europe, have given us marriage partners aplenty to play with.

These marriages arouse the interest and the professional curiosity of very few wine writers and critics. It was Maurice

Chevalier who so artfully pointed out that 'many a man falls in love in light so bad he wouldn't choose a suit by it', and so it is that many a wine critic judges a wine in conditions inappropriate to making judgements about its marriage with food. As candidates for partnering with food, wines in a professional wine-tasting are given no chance to demonstrate their suitability. The wine-taster must use imagination and skill to do this, and critics have enough on their plates coming to a simple decision about the nature of the wines in their glasses without venturing into the more exotic area of what sorts of food might go with them.

However, I must confess I rarely taste a wine without immediately thinking of the food it will go with, for it is with food that it is designed to go. Wine is not created solely to be compared with other wines and end up being spat into a metal bucket or a ceramic spittoon. It is for this reason that I taste many wines several times over, often with food to see whether my hunches are correct.

In this regard, it is undoubtedly true that the wine-taster's job is made more difficult nowadays because of all the different kinds of ethnic foods we enjoy in the UK. Old-style European wines do not accompany these foods as purposefully as the New World wines. The repertoire of wines available from UK retailers' shelves is now immense. Those wine critics (and there are some) who do not find Thai food or Indian cooking to their taste, are all at sea when it comes to finding the wines to go with them, for not only is the food uncongenial but the wines best suited to go with such foods are foreign to their palates.

> ❛ I must confess I rarely taste a wine without immediately thinking of the food it will go with, for it is with food that it is designed to go ❜

Luckily, I am greedy and impatient and fascinated by change and development, and so I am happy to throw all sorts of different foods at all kinds of wines to see what emerges. The wines and dishes below are the results of my dedicated search to find the perfect wine for the perfectly delicious dish, and I hope you enjoy yourself.

This is not an exhaustive survey: I have merely chosen certain traditional and modern favourites. Nor is it a set of rules which brook no contradiction: these are my ideas, not a set of instructions.

Marriage is dead, sayeth the cynic? It might be under question as a social institution in Britain, but as a gastronomic one involving food with wine it is alive and well and fully kicking.

Soups and starters (in general)

'*The servants had already brought in the soups, one made of beer, sugar and eggs, one of rose-hips and onions, one of bread and cabbage-water, one of cows' udders flavoured with nutmeg. There was dough mixed with beech-nut oil, pickled herrings and goose with treacle sauce, hard-boiled eggs, numerous dumplings. It is dangerous – on this, at least, all Germany's physicians were agreed – not to keep the stomach full at all times…*' Starters in 1795, as endured by characters in Penelope Fitzgerald's beautiful novel *The Blue Flower*, 1995.

I have one simple rule when giving the matter of which wine to serve with the first course any thought, and it is this: either serve the wine your guests are drinking as an aperitif or serve the wine you have chosen to go with the main course. This only runs into difficulties, or rather dictates certain responses, if the aperitif you have chosen is dry sherry (in which case ensure that grilled prawns are the first course) or a sparkling wine (in which case smoked salmon or smoked eel will do as a starter). But of course if you are starting with mussel soup and going on to pheasant casserole then you cannot contemplate either of these wines and therefore you should think in terms of a Chilean or New Zealand Sauvignon Blanc to begin with followed by a robust red Cotes du Rhone to follow.

Pea and ham soup

This brilliant broth, which can be made cheaply by using liquidized pea pods, invites a choice of wines depending on your mood. Its smokiness will suit a light, crisp partner in summer, a smooth red in winter. Thus you have a choice: a lightly chilled own-label **Chilean white** (Tesco, Safeway, Sainsbury and Asda, at around £3) or **South African Pinotage** from the same retailers (plus the Co-op, Thresher, Victoria Wine and Waitrose) at around £3.49.

Fish and chips

A clean white wine with a measure of crispness about it is needed here to counterbalance the batter. But fruit is also a requirement. A wine like Asda's **Newlands Chenin Blanc** (£2.69) is perfect, though this is a vigorously ripe and fruity number with its crisp, acidic side subdued until two or three hours after opening. The most sublime wine, especially if the fish is sole, skate or turbot, is Chilean Sauvignon Blanc – like **Santa Carolina** (Oddbins, £4.49) or **Concha y Toro** (Oddbins, £4.99).

Fish and red wine

Whole roasted sea bream with roasted fennel and a Barbaresco are a magical combination. Barbaresco, made, like Barolo, from the Nebbiolo grape in north-western Italy, is a light but rich red wine with a subtle edging of licorice. With the fish and the fennel it works brilliantly. Gaja makes stunning Barbarescos but so do Pelissero, Bruno Giacosa and Ceretto. Volvona and Crolla in Edinburgh have these wines, pricey but imperious. This merchant's telephone number is 0131 556 6066. Other good producers are de Gresy, Cigliuti, Traversa and di Neive. Oddbins had 1990 **Castello di Neive Barbaresco** for £7.99.

Roast beef

There has always been a natural affinity between rare roast beef and claret and it is not a union created solely out of

sentiment. There is a chemical reason for the success of the partnership due to the blood of the meat and the tannin in the wine. Who am I to gainsay nature? A fruity Cabernet Sauvignon with a handsome tannic shroud is my bottle, then, but it is not from France. It is Cabernet Sauvignon delle Tre Venezie (£3.99 from Italy and Sainsbury).

Other candidates include: **Castillo de Mont Blanc** (Fullers, £3.99), **Mexican Cabernet Sauvignon** (Tesco, £3.99) and **Rama Corta** (Victoria Wine, £3.49).

Steak and kidney pudding

My first choice here is unhesitatingly **Moroccan red**, on sale at just under £3 at Morrison, Safeway and Sainsbury. There is a rich, warming gaminess to the dish and so it is with the wine. Sadly, this alliance may soon be one of nostalgia, if sensitivity over eating beef is here to stay.

Roast lamb with mint sauce

Zlatovich Mavrud, around £3. Mavrud is a hugely unsung Bulgarian red grape variety, slanderously dismissed by several 'experts' as rubbish, and I welcome its emergence. In certain circumstances, it recommends itself over the classic wines grown in Bulgaria, like Cabernet Sauvignon, which have been widely sold and appreciated in the UK for twenty years. Mavrud is a wonderfully fruity red wine, of huge potential, greatly belying its reputation as a no-hoper. It has a certain rusticality, but with lamb with mint sauce bottles like **Zlatovrach Reserve Mavrud** 1990 (Sainsbury) and **Mavrud Reserve** 1991 (Waitrose) are worthy partners.

Kidneys in red wine sauce

Not your everyday sort of dish, but the ingredients are widely available and the matching of wine with such rich, gamy fare provoked a very revealing debate between myself and a *sommelier* in a very posh restaurant in west London – so I couldn't resist including it as an entry in this section on food. I am rarely given to patronizing such establishments, as I find the clientele upsettingly overripe and the food usually overpriced and contrived. But it was a celebratory occasion and I found myself sitting there as happy as a pig in mud once I had digested the wine list. What follows occurred word for word.

Me (holding wine list): I'd like a bottle of Mas de Daumas Gassac 1993.
Sommelier (a Frenchman in his prime): Oh, zir. Too zung to drink, I tink. Do zu know zis wine?
Me: Do you know what I am eating?
Sommelier: Er...erm...
Me: I will tell you. I am having the kidneys. They will go splendidly with the wine which is very young, as you say. Had you checked what I had ordered to eat you would know that the tannin in this wine will change and soften once the red wine sauce and those kidneys get to work on it. To answer your question, I do know the wine. I am surprised you list it, if you consider it too young to drink.
Sommelier (controlling his confusion brilliantly): Er...erm... Zank you, zir. I will get you your zwine immédiatement.
Me: And decant it, please.

Two things need to be said here: firstly, the Frenchman was a clot. He should not list a wine he advises customers is too young to drink and he should have checked what I had ordered before he announced himself at the table. I will say no more about him. Secondly, the wine went brilliantly with the food and was immeasurably helped by being decanted, and would have gained in softness and depth with the kidneys over several hours (had I spent that long eating and drinking).

I decant almost all red wines, and many whites, into a clean glass jug prior to serving. It is not enough to open the bottle to let the wine inside breathe. Air must get into all the wine, not just affect the few inches (or less) that are open to the air in the neck of a bottle. A fancy decanter is not necessary, it is not even desirable in most circumstances. I much prefer my fat glass jug which I rescued from duties as a household

> **❝ I decant almost all red wines, and many whites, into a clean glass jug prior to serving. ❞**

vase. It takes three bottles comfortably (and five at a pinch, but then it becomes rather a problem to hand around the table for people to pick up and pour for themselves).

▶ Mas de Daumas Gassac is from southern France and one of the profoundest red wines in Europe. It is not cheap, just under £10–£13 at various wine merchants and chains (Booths of Preston and Thresher), but it ages prodigiously well and with the right food is obviously fine drunk fairly young in its development. But it offers, when it gets over five or six years old (the wine will stay fighting fit for twenty years easily), an aromatic feast for the nose, a warm, deep treat for the palate, and a fiercely lingering finish for the throat that hints at spice and soft, dark, leathery fruits. The overall effect of the wine is one of sublime sensuality and rustic robustness with never a hint of coarseness. A wine of character? Indubitably. It has only Vin de Pays status but it is, for me, a vin merveilleux – a marvellous wine worth every penny.

Sausages and mash

Precisely what is this dish? I like it best with spicy sausages (and mustard on the side), mash which has been puréed with a little green olive oil, and onion gravy. In these circumstances, a rousing red will do the dish proud. The choice of bottles is as wide as the style of sausage you elect to fry (or grill or roast). My favourites are the new Merlot/Pinot blends coming out of Bulgaria and Romania under £3. Victoria Wine has the Bulgar (£2.99), Sainsbury the Romanian (£2.85).

Curries

With the exception of fish or prawn curries (with which you can utilize the wine referred to immediately below for chicken tandoori) the wine here is a rich, not too woody, delicately vanillaey Garnacha/Tempranillo from Spain. **Don Darias** in the old days used to be my favourite, but it has lost its excitement in recent years and so I would go for the £2.99–£3.49 examples of the grape like **Navajas Rioja** (Morrison, £3.29), **Puerto de la Villa** (Victoria Wine, £2.99) or **Puelles Rioja** (Oddbins, £3.49).

Chicken tandoori or tikka

A rich, rolling, oily Australian Chardonnay is the ticket here. My favourite is **Wolf Blass** (Oddbins, Co-op and Littlewoods, about £6).

Chinese takeaway

My favourite wine with this vivid sort of food is **Gewurztraminer d'Alsace** (various supermarkets and chains at £4.99). This is a deeply fruity wine, which is white though made from a rose-hued grape, and its subtle perfume is sometimes reminiscent of crushed rose petals and the

fruit of lychees. Some outstanding examples are: **Gewurztraminer d'Alsace, Cave de Turckheim 1994** (Somerfield), **Gewurztraminer d'Alsace, Turckheim 1994** (Safeway), **Gewurztraminer d'Alsace Beblenheim 1993** (Waitrose).

But if you want to lash out on more complex bottles, then the place to visit is Thresher's Wine Rack emporia. Here you can get the lovely **Zind Humbrecht Gewurztraminer 1992** (£6.99) and the **Gewurztraminer Herrenweg 1992** at £7.99.

Vegetable dishes

Vegetarian food is a label to shy away from. Yet do we not eat lots of vegetable dishes nowadays? Vegetables roasted in the oven with olive oil and whole garlic cloves are superb, and I regard mushroom risotto as a treat (yet economical enough to eat every day if you wish). These dishes are extremely filling and delicious. It is for this reason that I like a deliciously filling wine with them – like **Domaine de la Grande Bellane Valreas Cotes du Rhone Villages 1993** from Victoria Wine Shops and Cellars. This is a wine made from organically raised grapes in the village of Valreas, and its dry fruit is packed with flavour. It has a suggestion of spice, a light dusting of tannin, and a touch of wild herbs baked in the sun. At £5.99 it outgunned many fancier Cotes du Rhones I tasted in 1995 priced three and four times higher. I hope the '94 vintage is as good.

Bread and cheese

'...*he took care to include a yard of long French bread, a sausage out of which the garlic sang, some cheese which lay down and cried, and a long straw-covered flask containing bottled sunshine...*' The Rat's picnic in *The Wind in the Willows*, Kenneth Grahame, 1908.

But what was the wine? Obviously some perfectly dreadful Chianti – a wine of monstrous unpredictability in those days. Ratty had a deeply suspect palate where these things were concerned. I would prefer to drink with such food a red wine which flaunted plenty of bottled sunshine, to be sure, but more earthy oomph and unrefined rusticality (without one whit of rawness). A wine like **Concha y Toro Unfiltered Syrah 1995**, for example. Costing £4.99 at Oddbins earlier this year, this wine had

aroma, texture, fruit, beautiful balance and a rich, lingering finish, all helped by the fact that it was, as the label said, unfiltered. In other words, all the tiny bits and bobs left over from the skins, etc. had not been screened out, and the result of this gorgeous non-censorship was a full-blooded yet delicate wine of delicious leathery texture, unreservedly pure, fruity flavour and extreme elegance, plus great individuality and panache. Perfect with bread and cheese. I await with eager expectation the 1996 vintage of this wine which will arrive as this book is going to press.

Bread and butter pudding

Moscatel de Valencia, no question. This sweet white wine, costing between £2.99 and £3.79 in supermarkets and high street retailers, has lush, gorgeous fruit, reminiscent of marmalade, and it is to be preferred over many so-called 'world-class' dessert wines costing £20 to £75. Victoria Wine has a fine example, so do all the leading supermarket chains. Marks and Spencer has a more classically styled example which comes across like a Beaumes de Venise. Moscatel de Valencia works splendidly with Christmas pudding as well.

4 WHAT'S IN A NAME?

(THAT WHICH WE CALL A ROSE BY ANY OTHER NAME WOULD SMELL AS SWEET)

The answer, dear Ms Juliet Capulet, is everything – as far as the subject in hand is concerned. Is it not droll (also ironic, fantastic, magical) to reflect on the great power of the right word in the right place? Once Upon a Time a French word, or a German one, on a wine label stuck on a bottle emanating from anywhere *but* France or Germany and anywhere you please (Cornwall, Croatia, Tunisia – or even Egypt or Madagascar to drag in two of the world's least likely but genuinely accredited wine producers), offered a solid measure of reassurance to the intending purchaser. In those bad and baldly deceptive days Australian burgundy and South African hock were rampantly soliciting for business unblushing and unrebuked. Subtler frauds were also perpetrated: Leonay Rinegolde, eleven shillings and threepence the bottle at Peter Dominic wine merchants in 1965, came from the Barossa Valley, New South Wales, admittedly home to many immigrant Germans but about as far from the Rhine as you can get.

The reason for all this naughty nomenclature was simple and obvious: France and Germany (and in the case of sherry, Spain) were regarded as the world's premier producers of certain types of wine, and thus to borrow from their languages was to acquire something of their status, and this reflected favourably on your wine. It did not matter what words you chose as long as they *sounded* right. You could have got away with calling your cod burgundy, conjured out of rank Pinotage vines growing somewhere in the Cape of Good Hope or grenache festering in the New South Wales sun, *Clos de Poubelle*. Doesn't it sound perfect? It is! *Clos* means a single enclosed vineyard (or field of anything, buttercups even, for that matter) and a *poubelle* is a dustbin. I have no doubt that a wine so named would have achieved a measure of sales success, even if its maker, possessed of more *chutzpah* than most of his breed, owned up to the meaning of the name, as long as he quickly romanticized it with a glorious set of lies about its origins having to do with an ancestor.

> **❛ It did not matter what words you chose as long as they sounded right. ❜**

This fraud (jolly though it was) was ended when legislation passed some years ago illegalized the practice. This did not, however, stop brewers from trying to give their UK-brewed lagers – characteristically vile – Germanic and Continental-sounding names – a custom which, when it ran into certain difficulties (like no one would drink the stuff), was circumvented by adopting a new tactic: brewing a Continental lager under licence in the UK and calling it, apparently perfectly legitimately, by its original name. This was a ruse which permitted the advertising and marketing of the product to echo the lager's original homeland. It was a supremely successful concept.

The other trick is to contrive a product in the correct country of origin, thus permitting a nicely exotic

and reassuring title, but devote all
your energies to exporting it (in
some cases because no discriminat-
ing native would give it a moment's
consideration).

Piat d'Or, for example, is a
well-known wine brand in Britain
and its ingenious television com-
mercials are constructed wholly
around the proposition that the
French themselves not only enthusiastically lap up the wine,
which is indeed made in France, but regard it as sufficiently
prestigious to take to dinner parties in order to impress their
hosts. It would not do, then, I can truthfully report, to flourish
a bottle of Piat d'Or at any dinner party held adjacent to the
Channel ports, for in this area of France the hypermarkets
have been known to shelve the wine in the Foreign Wines
section, not the French, in the belief that it is not French but a
foreign body – in other words, they have never heard of the
wine. The Piat d'Or proposition is a cunning ploy aimed at
seducing innocent beginners. You may retort that only a complete British booby would be taken in, but the fact is that there
is hardly a UK supermarket which does not stock the wine.
True, its popularity is not what it was, but it is still convincing
sufficient numbers of nincompoops every day to make the
brand viable.

But Piat d'Or is facing a dinosaur-like future, it seems to
me. A generation of drinkers is reaching maturity which does
not reverence France as the world's choicest wine country,
and this is why there has been a revival of the cod foreign
name. But in a delicious reversal of roles (and of fortunes), it is
not the Aussies or the Croats who pinch French words but
the French (and Germans and others), who use English words
for wines which were produced elsewhere. It is sometimes
justified by the fact that a flying wine-maker, often Australian
or English or from New Zealand, has had a hand in vinifying

the wine. Who wants to sound French any more when the Frogs are a tribe universally reviled for setting off subterranean nuclear bombs and, worse, making too many duff wines or bottles which have fallen from their once proud perches? The vogue is for names which suggest that the wine has come from some New World vineyard – preferably one which was once under the aegis of the British Empire.

Long Slim Red and Long Slim White? Surely, aren't these lean but obesely fruity wines from Hugga Mugga in Victoria where the law finally caught up with those notorious sheep rustlers, the dastardly Long Slim brothers, and justice was meted out to them via a noose? Nope. These wines are not Australian. They are Chilean. And excellent drinking and superb value they are at around three quid a bottle each at the Co-op.

Is Skylark Hill somewhere to be found on the map of New Zealand? No way. It is a wine grown exclusively in the Languedoc (and available at Kwik Save for under three quid).

Ed's Red is not Californian (though the wine-maker is American) but hails from Roussillon. Echo Hill and Devil's Rock (admittedly geological features of the German landscape usefully translated into English) are, surprise surprise, from Germany.

> ❛ A generation of drinkers is reaching maturity which does not reverence France as the world's choicest wine country... The vogue is for names which suggest that the wine comes from some New World vineyard. ❜

There are now scores of these wines (and a fairly comprehensive list of the most drinkable follows). But by now you will have got my drift. Or have you?

Why do I, you might be asking, feel this subject is worth a chapter, however short and cursory? Because for the eagle-eyed bargain hunter – and herein lies my true drift – the use of New World monikers for wines grown in countries which do not have English as a primary language is a glaring clue, more often than not, to a downright bargain. The reason for this is not that the wine must necessarily be cheap but that it must necessarily follow certain modern wine practices in order to qualify for titular anglicizing. I cannot think of a single example of this new genre that is downright dull, most vary from good to very good indeed. So look out for these beacons on the shelves. They light the way (to a lighter pocket and some deep, rich fruit).

▶ **Other names to look out for include**

Bad Tempered Cyril Tempranillo Syrah 1994 (Co-op): Spain

Badger Hill Chardonnay 1993 (Safeway): Hungary

Bear Ridge wines at Victoria Wine (Tesco and Kwik Save): Bulgaria

Chapel Hill wines (Co-op, Sainsbury, Tesco, Thresher and Victoria Wine): Hungary

Cool Ridge Barrel Fermented Chardonnay (Thresher): Hungary

Deer Leap wines (Waitrose): Hungary

Deinhard Yello 1994 (Morrison): Germany

Gold Label Chardonnay VdP d'Oc 1994 (Marks and Spencer): Languedoc

Lakeside Oak Chardonnay 1994 (Waitrose): Hungary

Orchard Hill Country Wine 1994 (Waitrose): Hungary

Riva White 1993 (Oddbins): Italy

Seafish Dry, Rheinhessen 1993 (Morrison): Germany

Silver Swan Olazs Rizling, Balaton 1993 (Safeway): Hungary

Sparkling Deinhard Yello (Morrison): Germany

Steep Ridge Grenache/Shiraz VdP d'Oc 1994 (Kwik Save): Languedoc

Steep Ridge Chardonnay/Sauvignon VdP d'Oc 1994 (Kwik Save): France

Winter Hill VdP de l'Aude 1994 (Morrison, Waitrose and Fullers): Languedoc

Fair Martina white wine (Co-op): France

A JOB FOR A WOMAN

5

'I have chosen to write about women, because I am not one myself, and because I have always preferred to write about subjects which do not tempt me to believe that I can ever fully understand them, but above all because many women seem to me to be looking at life with fresh eyes, and their autobiographies, in various forms, are the most original part of contemporary literature. Their clash with old mentalities is the impasse which dwarfs all other impasses ...'
Theodore Zeldin, *An Intimate History of Humanity*

I have said it once. I have said it a thousand times. And I will go on saying it until gender is of no further importance in these matters.

Women, let me tell you, possess far more sensitive olfactory equipment than most men. I said *most*. Not *all*. There are tea-tasters, and whisky-blenders, and perfume-makers who are men and they all have extraordinarily sensitive eyes, noses and palates, and there are men blending sparkling wines in Australia, New Zealand and France who possess electrifying prowess when it comes to putting together the young wines which will harmonize and beautifully amalgamate over time to create one perfect wine. However, in the general run of things women, perhaps because they develop an early appreciation of smell, seem better equipped than many a man to judge wine. Maybe women's biological history has predetermined them to have more acute

❝ ... it is to women that much of the recent revolution in wine owes its origins and its continuing expansion. ❞

sensory organs where smell and taste are concerned.

This is informed speculation, but what is not is that it is to women that much of the recent revolution in wine owes its origins and its continuing expansion. Women, firstly, introduced men to the idea of supermarket shopping around the time that the revolution in information technology was beginning (1973) but it was not until the recent recession (which first flickered into life, if it is possible to date these things precisely, in late 1988 and was only declared on its last legs in late 1994) that men became practised supermarket shoppers, not only where wine is concerned but with many other products also. The recession finally concreted the supermarkets into position as the nation's leading wine retailers.

During this period women in the UK also drank so much white wine that they knocked bitter off its perch as the nation's favourite alcoholic tipple. Women also increasingly found employment as professional buyers of wine for the supermarkets and wine retailers and merchants. Women also now make wine all over the world in increasing numbers. It is an industry dominated by men, but women play a vital and burgeoning role in it.

Hungary is as good a place as any to start this investigation. Linguistically, indeed, it has no equal.

THE HUNGARIAN REVOLUTIONARY

Learning to communicate the right way in Hungarian, I discovered early on in my attempts to memorize merely a few basic courtesies, is not straightforward. I will provide an example. Ask the average Englishman if he knows the Hungarian word for woman and he will come back at you with the correct answer every time. He will say no. And that is the right answer. No.

What can one make of a language in which no is a woman (and bor means wine)? I regretted my inability to communicate most when I was in Kiskoros, a small town on the Great Plain between the Danube and Tisza rivers, where I first met Marta Domokos and recorded in my notebook: 'Today, I met a five-foot-nothing Hungarian no wine-maker. I was speechless.' I had wanted to tell her personally that her wines made the world a better place but I had to rely on an interpreter to do this for me. The fact that I was in the same boat (ugyanugy elkuld, in case you wondered) as the UK trade wine buyer with me was no consolation. The trade buyer made her feelings known by buying most of the wine Marta makes. I relied on deep sighs, large smiles, and several refusals to utilize the spittoons.

A typical Marta Domokos' red wine, metamorphosed from a 100 per cent local Kekfrancos grape variety wine in the tasting room to a niftily labelled Hungarian Country Wine on the shelf, is perfectly weighted with alcohol at around 11.5 per cent, alive and wriggling with young rounded fruit like some beaujolais of yesteryear, and has immense charm. Fresh with plummy flavours, with touches of smoke and rubber and a natural fruity finish, it is a delightful mouthful. To me it seems like beaujolais ought to be: fun, cheap, and running wild and free with fruit.

Marta's Chardonnays taste terrific, too. They typically show elegant, subtle touches of rich butter with a bitter-almond finish. Old-fashioned in style and structure and certainly not New World wines, but certainly individual. I was pleased to see Marta's delight at my nakedly enthusiastic appreciation of her wines. She let slip something I have never heard of before. Apparently, each grape variety in each tank has a secret code which only the wine-maker can decipher. 'Like a mother with the moods of her children,' she added.

Nowadays Ms Domokos has become something of a roving wine-maker if not a flying one. She oversees production at various wineries favoured by UK supermarkets (especially Liz Robertson's Safeway which discovered her first) and has an expanding empire of her own.

THE AUSTRALIAN REVOLUTIONARY

Mandy Jones's challenge was in south-western France. The Premieres Cotes de Bordeaux region is where Chateau Carsin is to be found along with its winery – as modern and as technologically up-to-date as any anywhere, and this is where Ms Jones lives, sleeps, eats, works, plays and makes wines. But a short jog down through the vines and there is the ancient village of Rions, a modern hot-spot itself in the twelfth century, whose inhabitants, once ruled by English kings and queens, are still governed by tradition, as is most of Bordeaux. Not surprisingly, the locals wondered about the tall Aussie female when she arrived at the Chateau on the crest of the slope (not to mention the new violin-playing owner of the place, Norwegian wine enthusiast Juha Berglund). What could she be doing here? A *woman* in charge of the wine-making? But Mandy's gender wasn't the biggest cause of local astonishment.

'What really surprised them,' Mandy told me, 'was that I came from Australia. "How come you know about wine, they asked me. Do they have vineyards in Australia?"'

Doubtless the locals haven't heard of Sainsbury or Waitrose either. But both stores have heard of and like the wine. **Chateau Carsin Bordeaux Blanc** (£5.50+) and **Chateau Carsin Premieres Cotes de Bordeaux Rouge**

(£5.80+) are on sale at Sainsbury, and Waitrose has the white which is called **Cuvee Prestige** (around £6). Other countries in Europe buy some, and the President of Finland takes two barrels a year. The white is crisp, nicely balanced, and elegant. The red is dry with a savoury tannic side integrated well with the rich, soft fruit. Both wines, it is fair to say, exhibit their provenance. But this Bordeaux typicity offers an unusual depth of polish and respect for the fruit over the wood. The white is mainly Semillon with Sauvignon Blanc. The red is Merlot and Cabernet Franc with Cabernet Sauvignon. Local recipes, both, but given added flavour and excitement by modern wine-making techniques and vine management.

Mandy is well seasoned and well travelled. She was born into a wine-making family thirty-five years ago, has studied at one of the most respected wine universities in the world (in Australia), once supervised the

❛ Do they have vineyards in Australia? ❜

laboratory for Taylor's Port in Portugal, and before she came to Carsin she was an assistant wine-maker at another Bordeaux property. She's also a regular student at a Saturday and Monday morning course at Bordeaux University. This both perfects her French (which was flowing and fluent when I met her at the Chateau) and helps her to understood more of local wine-making customs. As it happens, I strongly suspect she has as much to teach her teachers about wine-making as they do her, but she is far too polite to hint at such a thing.

The wines speak for themselves. But a woman working in a man's world (what woman *doesn't*, you might correctly point out, but let this pass) will often merely smile to herself and let you infer what you like. But I do know how men behave in small, closely knit situations and I regard Mandy as remarkably resolute to be seeing it through so supremely well.

Men will, for instance, take other men's expertise for

granted once the silliness of the customary male initiation rite is over. Women play no part in such rites so they have to work all the harder to prove they are worthy of dodging the trial. Such endemic prejudices where male–female relations at work are concerned are given added poignance in Bordeaux where women wine-makers are rarer than hen's teeth. But she's battled through the 'well done, little girl' sentiments to be seen as a tough and successful operator in her own right. The only culture shock she still finds it hard to come to terms with is the ritual of the two-hour lunch.

THE WEST LONDON REVOLUTIONARY

Liz Robertson, however, can come to terms with a two-hour lunch because she once bought me one – in a Sri Lankan restaurant on the Finchley Road in North London. Ms Robertson runs Safeway's wine-buying department from an office nor far from Heathrow.

I cannot imagine what it must be like to be an employee of a whopping great big supermarket. I have been emotionally self-employed for all my working life (and truly self-employed for twenty out of the past twenty-four years) so I'm not sympathetic to the idea of the corporate ethos. I am more struck by individuals than companies. And I am most struck by individuals who are just that: individuals. Individuals, above all, who are not mere servants of their company's philosophy but bosses of their own emotions and possessed of uniquely individual styles. Many of the men running wine-buying departments for retailers could swop jobs and no one would notice any difference, but Elizabeth Robertson MW has brought a special flavour to Safeway both through her admirable personality and keen intelligence and the way she has utilized both to satisfy the wine-buying needs of Safeway's customers.

Wine in a Tetrapak? That came out of Ms Robertson's

department first, and what a splendid pair the first wines so packaged were: Australian Shiraz and Australian Semillon the shape of fat paperbacks (and just as easy to stuff in the picnicker's pocket) but containing the same as a full 75-cl bottle, at £2.99 apiece.

Another of her department's initiatives was wine with strict vintage guarantees (so that customers would only ever get the latest vintage of a wine and not be palmed off with older vintages which would normally wait to be exhausted before the newer one was brought on).

Young vatted wines from Eastern Europe and Spain were another Safeway innovation also. **Young Vatted Cabernet Sauvignon** and **Young Vatted Merlot**, £2.99 each, were the first, and these superbly drinkable Bulgarian wines were followed by a Young Vatted Tempranillo (£3.49) from Spain. Other wines are in the pipeline. The concept has been to produce non-oak-aged wines with lots of supple, fresh fruit – bottled straight from the stainless-steel tank.

And what about the Wine Fairs the store puts on? These events, where specially purchased bargains proliferate, are a regular excitement for Safeway shoppers.

Ms Robertson, who is widowed with a teenage daughter, seems to me to be about fourteen years old herself at times, such are her energy and her abundant love of wine. It is also her commitment to solving the old problem of faulty wine which impresses this wine writer.

Who else could persuade Penfolds, the achingly masculine Australian wine company, to stick a vivid yellow plastic cork in a new wine? Will this innovation cure the problem of corked wines? Undoubtedly it will, for corked wine, that is to say wine which is faulty because it has been tainted by a microscopic chemical imperfection inside the cork, is the great single cause of dissatisfaction where wine is concerned and one of my own biggest bugbears (see Chapter 7 for more on this).

THE BAKER STREET REVOLUTIONARY

If we can congratulate Ms Robertson of Safeway for her plastic cork, we can congratulate Jane Kay of Marks and Spencer twenty times over. Ms Kay has been instrumental in developing the idea of plastic corks at Britain's best-loved high street retailer to the extent that twenty Marks and Spencer wines are now synthetically sealed.

'The only problem we've ever had in five years,' remarks Jane convincingly, 'is that a customer once told us that she couldn't for the life of her get the cork back in the bottle.'

Marks and Spencer, being exceedingly exercised at the thought of an aspect of quality control being outside its domain and subject to regular inconsistencies, hired Jane Kay some five years ago. She is the only trained oenologist (a scientifically qualified wine-maker) to be on the staff of a retailer's buying department and her experience includes making commercially available wines (in Corsica). Jane works at M&S's Baker Street head office with one other colleague, Christopher Murphy, and their joint style – swashbuckling, elegant, refined yet no-nonsense – though nominally recalling Torville and Dean is much more the avenging Steed and Mrs Peel. Jane is around thirty, very fond of Chanel No. 19, and has a delicious, lop-sided grin and a reluctantly athletic, almost shuffling gait which suggests strength of the martially artistic sort. The grin tends to be displayed when serious questions are on the table.

'Oh no, Malcolm, it isn't just the Old World wine-making

countries who find dealing with a woman in a traditional man's role difficult to handle. Some of the New World countries, they see someone fairly young and female turn up, and you can see from the immediate look on their faces, and I'm talking about men here, that they're thinking, "What on earth is this girl doing in this job?" Most telling is when their attitudes change half-way through the meeting. You're at a tasting and you've been treated quite superficially, and they think they can palm you off with some cock-and-bull story, or try to explain how good the wines you're tasting are when you don't think they taste terribly good, and you can sense the realization when suddenly they recognize that this person, this young woman, knows more than they thought she did, and they suddenly start to take you more seriously.'

She laughs. And why not? We are sitting together in a restaurant with a terrific view of the Thames and we're drinking Barolo. And I'm a man, too, so maybe she's thinking to herself, 'Why all these dumb questions?'

'Actually, I think the initial suspicion created by being a woman can be quite helpful in the long run. Because once you do get over the early stages and you've proved you know what you're on about, they'll help you and be on your side. They can become far more receptive to what you're asking for and more willing to listen

> **❛ ... it isn't just the Old World winemaking countries who find dealing with a woman in a traditional man's role difficult to handle. ❜**

and become effectively involved in, say, our blends and what we're looking for at M&S.

'Quite often when you talk to a cellarmaster he's quite defensive, he won't admit that things could be done differently. Or he's got something tucked away in his cellar he's reluctant to bring out. But once you get involved with them, they'll co-operate...'

'Seems strange they don't see you as another wine-maker

– with your oenological background….' I muttered.

'That doesn't really count for much. There are many people with scientific backgrounds and they don't get treated any differently. In France, for instance, I would say that wine-makers are treated with less respect and receive not as high esteem as someone in marketing or some of the commercial people.'

The difference, then, between the Old World of wine and the New is very marked?

'One of the biggest differences between the two is the openness and the willingness of the New World. It is much more marked. This even affects women. There are many women now making wine in France and they've had to work harder to make their mark and be more disciplined at keeping their team in order. I think there are a lot of male wine-makers who shouldn't be making wine in the first place. Certain men have their positions not because they are any good but because they were simply the right sex in the right place at the right time. Whereas women have had to prove their worth, and really merit respect because they have the talent and the application.'

Another gulp of the Barolo.

'And I'm not talking about old–established family wine companies here. Quite often it's the same in some of the French co-operatives. The father has handled the wine-making for eons and he simply hands on responsibility to the son. Even though he might not be the best person for the job. That's wrong.'

> **❛ I think there are a lot of male wine-makers who shouldn't be making wine in the first place... women have had to prove their worth, and really merit respect because they have the talent and the application. ❜**

I attempt to refill her glass. But the carafe is now empty. And I've run out of questions.

STAR TREK: THE GREAT WINE REGIONS OF THE TWENTY-FIRST CENTURY

6

'The best of Prophets of the future is the past.'
Lord Byron, letter, *28 January 1821*

S ome decades ago now there landed on the Hudson River dockside, in New York, an imported car which drew a laughing crowd and a sneering response, from the established US domestic automobile manufacturers, of 'No American will ever get inside it.' It was a silly-looking, unfashionably shaped car conferring no obvious prestige and offering meagre (by US standards) petrol consumption, startling reliability and an off-puttingly alien object sticking out of the floor called a gearshift. That car was the Volkswagen Beetle. The rest is history. Americans took to the car in such numbers it revolutionized the national attitude to what a motor car was, what it was supposed to achieve and how it could achieve it. The revered over-powered gas-guzzler with its emblematic fins and elaborate stainless steel superficialities was shown for what it

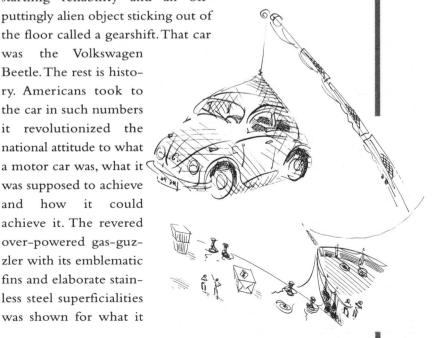

was: as hollow an icon as a painted totem. The US car industry, since then, has lost its monopoly of its home market and VW, Japanese and Swedish cars are as revered as apple pie.

The relevance of this story to the world of wine is dramatic. Wine merchants scoffed at the idea that their customers would ever patronize supermarkets. The notion that such establishments would attract serious wine drinkers was, surely, a joke. The newer, brasher wine shops, gaudy establishments like Oddbins, were also cause for amusement. (Even as I was writing this book, would you believe, a wine importer confided to me that the Oddbins approach to retailing wine was in his opinion unwise and farcical. 'All those juvenile scribbles over the window. Confuses customers, y'know.' I did not console him with my thought that I was sure his manifest talents would find an alternative avenue of expression when his own wine business went down the drain.)

The established wine regions of the world, certainly the most famous, also felt secure and scornful when New World wine regions began producing a wide variety of bottles for the first time in exportable quantities. The idea that a Sauvignon Blanc from New Zealand, for instance, would one day supplant one from Sancerre as the finest example of its type was uncountenanced; that the Spaniards could possibly create a sparkling wine to compete with champagne was to believe the moon was inhabited by little green men; and the proposition that Australian wine would ever end up on every single wine shelf in Britain was as fanciful and extravagant a suggestion as saying that one day in the near future the ordinary working individual would own a colour TV set and have a telephone by the bed.

Unthinkable, also, was the more recent discovery, to the horror of the marketing forces behind the old established regions, that own-label wines created specifically for individual supermarkets and wine chains would compete so strongly with their own bottles that it called into question the whole basis of what branded wine stood for in the UK. The British drinker has discovered value for money.

But what do I mean by a great wine area of the twenty-first century? I mean an area the wines of which will become, like the wines of Burgundy once were in days gone by, unequalled and famous. This potential may, of course, never be realized for much the same reasons that Burgundy's has been squandered. I can only hope otherwise (and do what I can to drink the wines as often as I can and write about them). It is, however, worth bearing in mind that there is a generation of drinkers growing up who are unacquainted with the notion of the greatness of some of the old established regions. They are already wedded to the idea that their Cabernets should come from Chile and their Sauvignons from Marlborough and their sparkling wines from Catalonia.

The new wine regions offer better value (that is to say, better fruit for less money) than the old regions. I have not visited all the regions I consider the most exciting and most capable of replacing the older regions in the affections of future drinkers, but I can tell which of them I think most likely to succeed.

Western Australia, especially the southernmost tip near the ocean, offers vast opportunities for future vineyard plantings. It is already making its mark with established vineyards producing Chardonnay, Sauvignon Blanc, Riesling, Merlot, Cabernet Sauvignon and other varieties, yet only the surface of this area has been scratched. Hawkes Bay in New Zealand also has the resources, especially for Merlot and Cabernet Sauvignon, to match the reputation of its more famous cousin, Marlborough.

Hungary is opening up fast and the old by-words such as Bull's Blood and Tokay are being supplanted by Hungarian country reds and whites, various varietal efforts from individual wineries (often masterminded by imported winemakers), and the future is rich with promise. Romania offers the same prize (although it may seem crazy to think of such an old Roman province, the conquering of which is celebrated by Trajan's great column in Rome, as a New World wine country, the fact is that in attitude and expression it now is). Other Eastern European wine areas of established antiquity and full of new discoveries include Moravia (part of the old Czechoslovakia, see page 52) and Moldova – just across the Romanian border and part of both the old Bessarabia and the USSR. I exempt Bulgaria from this list because it has already substantially arrived, having started to develop its wine industry in the mid-1960s, well ahead of other countries.

Puglia in Italy is also ancient yet vibrant with new ideas, foreign influence and superb home-grown fruit. Sicily has promise, too. Navarre in Spain is also interesting.

And what of Oregon and Washington State on the Pacific coast of the USA? Exciting future famous wine areas without doubt if they continue their commitments to producing first-class fruit and conscientious wine-making practices. The area in California south from San Francisco Bay, the Santa Cruz mountains, is also an interesting, smaller region producing one of the world's greatest red wines from Ridge vineyards (see Chapter 13 for more on this wine). Baja California (Mexico), as represented by the wines of L. A. Cetto, is also up and running with wild fruit and as yet we have seen only a fraction of what this area can produce. Chile, too, is an area of yet-to-be-fully realized potential and is putting in place a formidable wine industry.

> ❛ The new wine regions offer better value (that is to say, better fruit for less money) than the old regions. ❜

But the two regions of the biggest potential have been producing wines for centuries: Catalonia in Spain and the Côtes du Roussillon in southern France. The first you undoubtedly know about since you've probably enjoyed Cava, but the second? Well, even the travelled wine hack has some difficulty locating it and pin-pointing exactly where it is. And the wines? Hold on. We'll get there all in good time.

WESTERN AUSTRALIA

'*...that air of owning the city which belongs to a good Australian*'.
D. H.Lawrence, *Kangaroo*, 1923

Peter Dawson was the first wine-maker I slept with and I must say he was terrific in bed. He didn't snore once and if he sleep-walked it certainly didn't rouse me from my slumbers. But then I was lying on the only proper mattress in the room. He had the flimsy camp bed. We had flipped a coin for who got which and he called tails when the smart call was heads. I advise any traveller intending to stay in Pemberton, Western Australia, especially if you have reserved a room in the town's only motel, to be warned: it is wise to phone before you arrive, even if you have

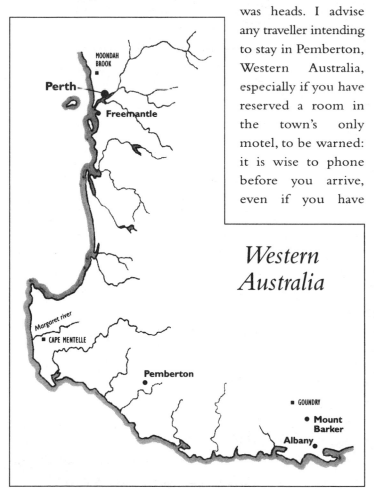

Western Australia

confirmed by letter and fax, otherwise you may lose your booking and your bed. In Western Australia they are a casual lot – wine-makers excepted. (I noted that Peter's bedtime reading was a scholarly tome on the chemistry of the Cabernet Sauvignon grape: he was boning up prior to delivering a lecture on the subject in a week's time.)

Nobody writes books about Western Australia. South Australians, Victorians and the New South Welsh, who produce the most famous wines in the land, are somewhat ignorant of this vast region. It is merely the world's biggest sheep station as far as they are concerned, and the wines which are grown there, apart from some of the more established ones grown around Perth, seem to be regarded as curiosities set beside the world-conquering products of the Barossa, Coonawarra and Hunter Valleys, or the Yarra. But be warned! This is a place to watch. The little bit I was in, the Indian Ocean one side, the Southern ocean the other, is right down on the southern tip of WA and the climate is perfect – hot days and cool nights – and the soils and drainage conditions suit viticulture perfectly.

Peter Dawson is the head honcho, where wine-making is concerned, of the BRL Hardy Wine Company of Australia. It was he who picked me up from my Perth hotel, twenty-four hours after I landed, thus generously giving me a whole day to myself to recover from the delicious exertions of Thai Airline's twenty-seven hour flight from London (stopover three hours in Singapore).

Australians are a sticky bunch. They club together and help each other. In Europe the mutual disaffection between some wine regions and neighbouring villages, even when they speak the same language and only

> ❛ **Western Australia... is a place to watch... the climate is perfect – hot days and cool nights – and the soils and drainage conditions suit viticulture perfectly.** ❜

fifty kilometres separate them, is as virulent as the ignorance and suspicion of those medieval dukedoms and minor royal fiefdoms which the area was once peppered with. So although Peter was my guide he wasn't sticking exclusively to his own company's wines, he was also showing me other people's and introducing me to their wine-makers and vineyards.

I'm pleased he showed me Moondah Brook vineyard, the eponym of the white wine widely on sale in the UK, for it was a particularly beautiful sight. An epidemic of arum lilies festooned both sides of the Brook itself and though these exotic blooms present a narcotic danger to any stock (cows and sheep) which might be tempted to take a bite they were, to this traveller's eyes at least, a feast. Peter also introduced me to Hardy's so-called **Houghton White Burgundy**, or HWB as it is labelled, a brand first made in 1937. It is Australia's most popular white wine. I confess to loathing one country stealing another country's wine names and so I was quite prepared to rate Houghton White Burgundy revolting, but Peter's pride in it pushed a glass my way and I found it rich, full and delicious and certainly reminiscent of a decent burgundy in flavour and structure. For a couple of quid a bottle (in Australia) it's one of the best white wines I'd tasted and the only disappointing thing about it is that the latest vintage, 1994 (Oddbins, £5.49), has become rather mushy and exotically fruity and has none of the classic hallmarks of the '93 and the '92 which were the first vintages to be exported here.

▶ **Moondah Brook wines available in the UK**

Moondah Brook Verdelho 1993 (Victoria Wine)
Moondah Brook Verdelho 1994 (Waitrose)
Moondah Brook Chenin Blanc 1993 (Victoria Wine)
Moondah Brook Chenin Blanc 1994 (Co-op)
Moondah Brook Cabernet Sauvignon 1991 (Booths and Safeway)

Expect to pay between £5 and £6 for these wines.

Moondah Brook and HWB are Swan Valley wines. This is where the Western Australian wine industry got started in 1829, a few years ahead of Victoria and South Australia. It is in the Margaret River area, however, that Western Australia exhibits its newest potential. Already some of its wines are beginning to find favour with the larger UK wine retailers. My favourites are Goundrey Estate Chardonnays, which Asda was the first big retailer to stock in the UK, and the Chardonnays made by mother Diana and daughter Vanya Cullen at Cullens.

▶ **Good SW Australian names to look for**
Capel Vale
Leeuwin Estate
Evans and Tate
Cape Mentelle
Ironstone
Sandalford
Vasse Felix
Plantagenet
Moss Wood
Alkoomi
Frankland Estate
Pierro
Wignalls
Goundrey
Cullens

Diana Cullen, who now takes a bit of a back seat to daughter Vanya where wine-making is concerned, told me that her own Margaret River vineyard was 'founded on scientific evidence to be a perfect microclimate for grapes. We were growing lupins! We've always liked wine and so ... hey presto! We have a vineyard.' The ex-lupin allotment is now twenty-five years old as a vineyard.

Oddbins have been partial to Cullens' wines. The 1995 Sauvignon Blanc, rich and very ripe, cost around a tenner. There's a Chardonnay at the same price. Adnams had a Cullens Cabernet/Merlot 1993, same sort of price, and this was deliciously spicy and warm.

Goundrey ships several wines to its UK distributor (Stratford's of Cookham in Berkshire, tel. 01628 810606) and these include **Mount Barker Chardonnay 1995** at Asda and **Mount Barker Riesling** at Morrison. Playford-Ross, merchants of Sowerby in Yorkshire, have the **Mount Barker**

Cabernet Merlot 1993 and the **Mount Barker Shiraz 1993**. Prices all under a tenner.

The most ambitious winery set up in the area is Cape Mentelle which is part of the Cloudy Bay business in New Zealand (or rather, it's the other way round since Mentelle has been going since 1969 and then expanded to NZ). The red wines are superb. The most exciting, alas, is not available in the UK. This is the Zinfandel, grown in a six-acre plot which just happens to be Australia's largest planting of the grape. It is a wine, in the '91 manifestation I tasted, as rich as blackberry jam.

David Hohnen, wine-maker and entrepreneur, said to me that he sometimes thinks of Margaret River as an island, and I know what he means. It is an area on its own, surrounded by the elements. This only increases the individuality of its wines and its wine-makers and enhances its status, in my eyes at least, as an area of spectacular potential.

There are four Cape Mentelle wines available in Britain. A Semillon/Chardonnay 1995, a Chardonnay 1994, a Cabernet/Merlot 1993 and a Shiraz 1993. These wines are variously stocked at selected branches of Oddbins, Wine Rack, Majestic Wine Warehouses, Davisons and Fullers. London merchants like Lea and Sandeman, Corney and Barrow and Berry Bros and Rudd also have them. Regionally, Adnams, Lay and Wheeler, The Nobody Inn, Great Western Wines, Bentalls, Tanners, Averys, Weavers, Connollys and Peckham and Rye in Glasgow go for the wine. Prices vary between £9 and £12. Good hunting!

HUNGARY

'*Such wines are fit for a pope.*' Pope Pius IV, 1562

The first thing I learned when I visited Hungary is that guide-books should contain shrink-wrapped pinches of salt

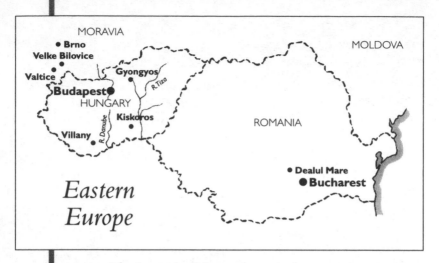

to enable the reader better to savour the contents. I had been assured by both guide- and wine-book writers that Hungary has a brand of cigarettes called Medoc Noir and I was keen and curious to purchase a packet, although I do not smoke. However, every single Hungarian I spoke to, even those who man (and woman) tobacco kiosks, denied absolutely the existence of such a tobacco product. It turned out to be the first of only two disappointments during my entire visit there. My second is explained by the following exchange.

'You cannot see our great castle in the fog,' said the driver as we puttered slowly over the bridge across the Danube which links Buda with Pest. "I'm sorry. It is spectacular. You would have enjoyed seeing it.'

'It's a great pity. I was looking forward to seeing this building I've heard so much about.'

'No matter,' said the driver eagerly, 'I will describe it to you.' And he did. At length. In hideous detail. I was spared nothing. But it's not the same thing as actually seeing the thing and it is also nerve-racking to be piloted in thick fog by a story-teller who periodically turns around to check that his audience is still awake and makes gestures with both hands during especially dramatic parts of his tale. Hungarians are very friendly people, anxious you should get the full picture.

Full everything, in fact. Never more so when it comes to food and wine. I tried to concentrate on the history of Buda Castle but I could not entirely rid my mind of the wonderful meal the previous night which was composed of goose liver accompanied by old Tokay wine (as curiously bitter-sweet as treacle topped with a dollop of Seville orange marmalade) followed by a pike with beetroot salad with an old Sauvignon Blanc. The richness of the food vied with the honeyed chords of the zither player and his colleagues who included a violinist, a cellist and a viola player. They were all drunk as skunks and plugged away on their instruments during the entire meal.

On the drive to this restaurant from the airport, my host's concern for my stomach was such that I was not allowed to check into my hotel first because the kitchen in the restaurant closed early on Sunday evenings. I had noted not a soul on any street anywhere and barely a single motor car. Now, even in this enveloping morning fog, the roads and pavements were buzzing. The pedestrians were marginally faster than the cars and they also seemed a good deal less vulnerable – especially where the Trabant, Eastern Europe's infamous automobile, was concerned. Over my scrambled egg and peppered sausage breakfast I was told that the Trabant is so unstable a vehicle that if it strikes a kerb at speed it can topple over and slide along the cobbles on its side, sending up sparks on which pedestrians have been known to warm their hands as the car passed by. I cannot claim to be disappointed I did not witness personally such a phenomenon because I have a feeling it's a story, unlike the Castle's, which is better told than experienced.

And I'd heard lots of stories about Hungary. Gyongyos, of course, figured largely in some of these because it was in this unobtrusive coal town, in 1990, that Englishman Hugh Ryman, son of the retired stationery magnate, first produced his attractive, irritatingly inexpensive Chardonnay. It put lots of people's noses out of joint, that wine. It wasn't the aroma, or the fruit, or its absurd provenance. It was jealousy. How was it possible for an Englishman, admittedly one who studied in Bordeaux and trained in Australia, to pitch up here and turn out such handsome wine for peanuts?

In fact, I wasn't due to meet Hugh on this visit but his man on the spot at the time, Adrian Wing, an Australian wine-maker built and coloured like a large rose trellis. Adrian would be recognizable on the streets of Gyongyos from a light aircraft a mile high not only because of his height, ruddy Aussie colouring and red hair but because he always carries a mobile phone as big as a TV set. To make amends for his charmingly egregious appearance and for bypassing the appalling insuffi-ciencies of the Hungarian phone system, he is engaged to a Hungarian woman and even speaks some Hungarian (now he is married to the former and on good terms with the latter, though by 1996 he was no longer working for the Ryman set-up). Sitting in the Gyongyos winery's meeting room where I met him, he was an exotic bloom amongst the chipped, grey, utterly expressionless Eastern European furnishing.

I am seated at a very long table about to taste wine from bottles which have been filled from the storage tanks. It is no ordinary tasting. The air is alive with friction, to which Adrian is utterly indifferent. Wouldn't you think that the winery director, sitting at the other end of the table simmering in his

grey suit, glowering beneath his flecked charcoal moustache, mentally spitting fire as forcefully as he will dutifully spit out the wines after tasting them, would be over the moon at the pioneering success of the Chardonnay? Not a bit of it. He, so he tells me through my interpreter, makes much better wines, and the Australian's are just a flash in the pan. Just a temporary fashion blip. You will agree, I am told, once I taste his wines.

Adrian is independent of this director but etiquette dictates I taste the director's wines first. I cannot quite get my mind around the idea that this grey-suited bureaucrat, having suffered two revolutions in a short space of time (the first political, the second vinous), has allowed foreigners in to make wines for export to the UK but continues to make his own wines in the old way. I taste the wines. I spit them out. A leading supermarket wine buyer also present at this unusual event also tastes and spits. You cannot read anything from our expressions. We are Englishmen. We do not box the ears of respectable middle-aged men merely because their wines taste and smell as if they had recently been used to boil root vegetables.

The UK trade buyer, however, whispers in my ear. 'Typical East European cabbagey flavour,' he says, 'with weak varietal characteristics and of no interest to the UK market.'

The director smiles when some semblance of this is passed on to him by the interpreter who may, for all I know since my grasp of the language is zilch, have lied through her teeth and reported that the UK trade buyer thinks the wines compare very favourably with the great white burgundies of Montrachet. We are later told that the director confidently believes the Japanese will go ape over his wines once they taste them. (This, of course, may well be true. The Japanese are on a planet of their own when it comes to alcoholic drink. I've seen Japanese clients of a New York sushi bar attack each other with sharp slivers of raw fish after the waitress gave one man the other man's bottle of Chivas Regal.)

Gyongyos Chardonnay, selling at around £3.50 at major UK retailers including Sainsbury, Safeway, Victoria Wine, Thresher and other high street wine shops, is fruity and stylish. It's not as good as it was. Maybe the winery director is right. But what actually makes it different from the old way of making wine? How does the New World of wine differ from the old?

I once asked Jacques Lurton, a thirty-something Frenchman from an old Bordeaux wine-making family who now makes wines all over the world, these questions. He has a foot in both camps, new and old, and he is able uniquely to sum up the basic differences between the two wine-making techniques.

'Okay,' said Jacques, smiling a broad smile and scratching the side of his magnificent Roman nose. 'You have to remember first that wine is 88 per cent water. That's the start of the recipe for all wines. Now, the Old World of wine is using the oxidized technique which loses some of the fruit character from this water. The New World is using the reductive technique. Reductive means without oxygen, unaerobic. This technique expresses very much the fruit character in the juice because it keeps more fruit in. That is the basic difference between the two worlds.'

The difference between the Old World of wine at

Gyongyos, as made by the director, and the New World of wine, as made by Hugh's colleagues (Adrian having since departed), is radically demonstrated when you taste the wines side by side. The Old wine is simply not as fruity, as rich, as fresh on the palate as the New. It seems flabbier, more wrinkled; it limps a little where the New wine strides out confident and bold. Part of the reason for this, which Jacques did not explain, is that New World white wine-making techniques keep grapes cool and the must which they create is always chilled. Why? It all helps to keep the fruit in the juice. Hugh Ryman once demonstrated the principle behind this to me when he took several grapes, cut them open, and left half of them on the kitchen table and placed the other half in the fridge. Tasted a while later, the grapes on the table were fruitless but the ones in the fridge had retained much of their natural freshness.

Gyongyos, of course, is a relative newcomer to the Hungarian wine scene and hardly the most famous. Tokay is the most renowned of Hungarian wines even though its quality suffered under the regimes since the war, and only recently have attempts been made to bring the wine back to its former glory. This intensely sweet wine, made mostly from the local grape, the Furmint, is legendary, a favourite at royal courts throughout Europe in the nineteenth century when it was considered acceptable for princesses to indulge in white wine – red being a man's drink, rough and heady. Typical social prejudice at work here, blatantly over-laden with chauvinist ignorance. For sweet white wine is, in fact, almost invariably stronger in alcohol than red but it doesn't seem that way.

> ❛ You have to remember first that wine is 88 per cent water. That's the start of the recipe for all wines. ❜

Perception, however, counts for so much where wine is concerned. It is perception, rather than reality, which forms the absurd basis of the ignorant prejudices which have maintained the status of many putative great Western European wines. For years, Eastern Europe, one or two exceptions like Tokay apart, was regarded as no place either to grow grapes or make wine. This despite the fact that much of the region enjoys a mild, almost Mediterranean climate, and an area like Hungary's Lake Balaton, for example, is a great place to site vineyards and also to find conscientious farmers with the skill and the will consistently to husband first-class crops of valuable wine grapes.

And here the flying wine-maker has landed and flourished also. Since the success of the Gyongyos Chardonnay and its Sauvignon Blanc Hungary has become riddled with the blighters, much to local delight, and near to the shores of the great lake a New Zealander called Warren Gibson is busily introducing the Magyars to antipodean wine wizardry. Balaton is Europe's biggest lake and it appears at first sight to be a crude mixture of Coney Island and the Lake District. Tradition has made the lake a mecca for holidaying Hungarians, not to mention Austrians, for many generations, though when I first went there it was in the depths of winter and not a sunshade was to be seen.

Picture the surreal absurdity of the scene as I descend to the winery and gaze up at the tanks of wine. It is 2.25 in the afternoon. It is below freezing and eleven people are grouped around a drain grille set in the floor of the storage tank cellar. They are all wearing overcoats (and I'm glad I thought to pack my thick Scottish woollen sweater) and they are all spitting, the expectorations sending out clouds of breath from every pair of lips. I am invited to join them. An hour goes by. An hour of steamy slurping, tasting, spitting, gargling. The cold settles in the folds of my sweater and begins to prick my skin. I haven't had a bite of lunch yet. I'd love a mug of malt whisky-fortified steaming tea.

This is the glamorous life of the international wine writer?

We taste dozens of different wines straight from the tanks. A flurry of mystical remarks falls:

'Muscat is delicate. It changes faster than anything.'

'A wine shows itself up front then grows a tail as it ages.'

'Is there enough aroma here to see us through?'

'How reductive is this wine? Will it improve measurably?'

In the end it comes down to five tanks of the latest vintage Chardonnay. More slurping takes place. By common consent, three recipes are written down and agreed:

50% of tank 1 and 50% of tank 3.

75% of tank 2 and 25% of tank 5.

25% of tanks 2 & 3 and 75% of tank 4.

Et voilà! We have three contenders for the perfect Hungarian Chardonnay! 'Send us the blends bottled and we'll think it over,' says the UK trade buyer. The Hungarians are all smiles.

This visit is remarkable for two further things. First, I persuade the supermarket buyer to consider taking a sparkling wine other people have said is rubbish but which I consider brilliant value for money. (And which, some months later, not only ends up on the supermarket shelves but also wins a silver medal at a wine show.) Second, I am witness to the first real bargaining session between buyer and seller to which I've ever been privy. To be sure, I've been around supermarket buyers when they've tasted wine they wish to consider purchasing, but this time there was no pussyfooting about. If this winery was going to do business with the UK then it was going to have to recognize the facts of life. "The price you would force us to sell your Chardonnay at is as much as an AC wine from the south of France. The British consumer won't stand for it, whatever the quality of your wine," said the trade buyer firmly. East European wine pricing has, apparently, its Scylla and Charybdis; they are the Vaucluse and the Luberon – get stuck between these two rocky Provençal wine areas, pricewise, and you're in trouble. I could not for a moment pretend to understand a word of this, nor have I upon deep reflection afterwards, but I do understand that the supermarket ends up with some terrific wines at incredibly low prices. But at least the lesson is over and I can get out of this cellar into the fresh air.

It's not the only lesson of my trip. As I bed down in the winery guest house I'm provided with an interesting insight into Hungarian plumbing. On the wall in the bathroom, beneath the mirror and above the sink, is a notice. It says 'Please open hot tap before you wish to use it as water take 4–5 minutes to appear'.

The Nagyrede winery I visited next morning and the Bataapati winery after that, owned by the Antinori family of Chianti fame, are both quiet and uneventful except for some momentary excitement at a superbly fresh and aromatic Tramini which excites me. Alas, I will be the one and only British wine drinker to enjoy this delightful aperitif-style wine – in seventy-two hours it will be on its way to the Rhine valley to be turned into Sekt. Bye bye, Tramini. Hello, hello, German sparkling wine.

In Bataapati I am in the rustic heart of Hungary and some of the village dwellings, unelectrified and dark, can't have changed their demeanour much in centuries. The best-maintained edifice in Bataapati, even more than the modern winery, is the First World War memorial with its gold paint gleaming like new though its inscriptions tell of an empire, the Austro-Hungarian, dead for nearly eight decades.

At Villany town, my interpreter suggests we stop for soup. We need something bracing before we reach the Villany winery itself, I'm advised, because we have a lot of wines to taste. Surprisingly, Adrian Wing turns up at the winery, in his capacity not as wine-maker but as adviser on certain aspects of the bottling of the Villany co-op wines. He astonishes the UK trade buyers also assembled here by taking out a glass phial and blithely adding copper sulphate to the Kekaporto grape variety wine in our glasses, to 'put some guts in it'.

Adrian adds: 'I copper everything. It's illegal, but we do it anyway. Well, in Bordeaux they achieve the same effect by hanging silver spoons in the barrels.' A moment later he adds, 'Only joking' (and he was), seeing the appalled expressions on the trade buyers' faces (who are mindful that a journalist is in the room with them).

It quickly becomes apparent, joke or no joke, that no British trade buyer has any intention of being a willing witness to the marriage of copper sulphate and wine, and the subject, and the phial of sulphate, is quickly dropped.

'I hate to bring up something so tasteless as price,' puts in a buyer, and I'm back on familiar territory. I find from my notes that the new vintage Kekfrancos grape variety wine seemed to me to be 'raspberryish and nutty, dry and well shaped' and I added the proviso that 'any mucking about by Australian chemists with boxes of tricks' should be avoided like the plague.

When, some months later, in Australia itself, I recounted my Hungarian adventures to a group of wine-makers, I was surprised by the vehemence with which they dismissed the Hugh Ryman operation and the flying wine-maker concept. 'Ryman takes raw cellar hands, gives them recipes from which they can't deviate, and packs them off to some Third World winery the other end of nowhere and they call themselves wine-makers. Damn ridiculous,' said one famous Aussie oenologist. Ryman will say that this is nothing but ignorant jealousy talking, that his wines have outstanding qualities which speak for themselves, and whilst his wine-makers may be young and relatively inexperienced this is what he's looking for in candidates for the job. Amusingly, the wines of one of Ryman's most outspoken critics were themselves dismissed as 'designer rubbish of no account whatsoever' by a London wine merchant in conversation with me, and all this proves is that the wine trade can be just as bitchy as any other.

Ede Tiffan, whom I met in the dark by the side of a Hungarian marsh I could not see, needs no lessons from anyone about wine-making. He's made wine sold in the UK for a few years past and he's in business just down the road from the Villany co-operative.

'This is a typical Villany Kekaporto,' he says to me as we sit down in the front room of his house. He hands me a glass of wine still going through its malolactic fermentation. (This secondary fermentation is discussed in more detail on pages 59–61). In hot, dry years like '92, he tells me, 'Only the good wine-makers managed to preserve acidity,' and the wines of that year are 'soft, too soft maybe, low in tartaric acid'. Without some acid a wine is all flab. It is in the control of the malolactic fermentation, whether a wine goes through a full 100 per cent one or is stopped by a technique which allows only a partial ferment to take place, that many wine-makers establish the final style of their wine.

With Ede, I'm in a world apart from flying wine-makers and stainless-steel tanks, and this feeling is greatly amplified when later I enter a barrel-lined, earth-floored cellar and taste wines of such rustic completeness and uncompromising typicity of style that I feel quite rejuvenated. I energetically nod my head with great enthusiasm but only after checking with Ede that this is the right response. I recounted to him the story of the UK trade buyer who caused massive confusion in Bulgaria on her visit to that country when she expressed a liking for a wine with vigorous nods of her head, only to discover that the Bulgars shake their heads when they mean yes and nod their heads when they mean the opposite. The Bulgars were utterly mystified when she bought loads of the wine.

> ❝ You must spend your life married to your grapes. ❞

Mystification is always lurking in a corner, waiting to pounce, where wine is concerned. When later I reached the town of Mor, where I enjoyed a wonderful evening with Istvan Gruber in his 250-year-old cellar, he adds to my store of mystification by saying, 'You must spend your life married to your grapes.' I felt sorry for the wife of this retired factory worker, now full-time wine-maker, for when I tasted his eight-year-old Tokay the love with which it was crafted shone all the way through every dizzily delicious drop. When the local TV station interviewed me I remarked that paradise would be to retire to Herr Gruber's cellar, marry his younger daughter, and bring little grapes into the world. My interviewer struggled, I sensed, to translate this for his audience.

Just as well, too, that some of the remarks I have made to my notebook during my Hungarian trip are not exposed on television. What could I have meant by writing, 'This man has a palate so refined you could hold a rugby scrum on his tongue and he wouldn't notice'? And who during my visit to Hungary could I have been referring to? What does 'an interesting murder' mean precisely in connection with one winery's attempt faithfully to vinify a particularly tricky grape variety? One note reads: 'A nondescript little wine of no special merit particularly well suited to non-celebratory occasions', with the rider that 'this note should be forwarded to whichever UK retailer buys the wine for use as a back label'.

> ❛ Hungary is now a major player on the world wine scene... ❜

Seriously, however, Hungary is now a major player on the world wine scene, and no one, especially the French (many of whose wines have been squeezed off the shelves by Hungarian bottles), is laughing. Except the Hungarians, perhaps, whose oblique sense of humour, refined through years of political aggression by clumsy outsiders, allows them to react to most things with a tight smile of ironic appreciation.

CATALONIA (DON'T INSULT IT BY COMPARING IT WITH BURGUNDY OR CHIANTI)

The more I think about it, the more I realize Catalonia is a great wine region NOW. A region which bears comparison

Catalonia

with some of the most famous in the world. NOW. Yet who thinks of Catalonia, with its three important constituent areas of Penedes, Costers del Segre and Conca de Barbera, as an even more diverse, an even more exciting, an even more fruitful area than the world-famous Burgundy or Chianti or even, from the same country of Spain, Rioja? Yet it is already one of the greatest wine regions in the world because it provides us with not only one of the great bubblies of the planet, Cava, but an abundance of white and red wines of increasing stature. It does more than compare with more renowned regions, it outpaces them. For Catalonia not only has some superb places to grow grapes, it also has significant individuals to raise that fruit and turn it into wine.

The cleverest Catalonian I know grows 150 different grape varieties. But has he got his hands full? Not by his own prodigious standards of output, interest, culture, and self-will. Señor Miguel Torres, a man I have learned to call Miguel, is based in a town a half-hour's drive from Barcelona called Vilafranca del Penedes. Miguel has time to oversee Spain's largest independent wine company, learn Japanese (in addition to his French, English, Spanish and Catalan), write food and wine articles and books (including an encyclopaedia), have the final say on the wine production front for the Torres owned vineyards in Chile and California, and play a mean game of tennis on his local club's orange clay courts. He is also the driving force behind the style of all the company's wines, their blending, and the techniques employed in growing the grapes on the 2500 acres directly owned by the business and the grower-owned vineyards which supply additional fruit. In 1994, the company sold seventeen million bottles of wine and seven million bottles of brandy to eighty-five countries. In some secrecy it also, last year, acquired the Jean Leon vineyards and winery. This Catalonian producer has produced French-style Cabernets and Chardonnays since the mid-1960s.

When I first met Miguel Torres, on a sultry afternoon at Expo-92 in Seville, he was neat and dapper in his suit and tie and he carried a furled umbrella like an extra limb. (An umbrella! In Seville! In summer! Incredible! Insouciant!) I was wearing sweat like suntan oil. I hated him. He had no right to be so cool and collected, and a year later he would remain equally unruffled under the onslaught of my serve and volley (an extravagant, illadvised tactic on clay but I was desperate).

The 150 varieties he grows are experiments in viticulture and grape selection and many of the old

> **❝ Catalonia... does more than compare with more renowned regions, it outpaces them. ❞**

Catalan varieties have enjoyed a flourishing new life in his nursery vineyard. This is not an indulgent hobby. This is a serious investigation into the suitability of various grapes for the soil and the climate and an equally serious project into the future. True, the money is made by all those bottles of wine the Torres company sells worldwide, and its reputation is made by the more expensive of these offerings, but who is to say that over the next few decades the likes of Garrut and Garnacha Negre, grape varieties no one except Miguel is growing and making into wine, will not, like Chenin Blanc or Merlot, become commercial realities either on their own account or as components in blends? I found both these varieties, when I tasted them as singly vinified varieties, exciting and hugely promising.

Just like Catalonia itself. The exuberance of Barcelona, from its great pre-war architect Gaudi to its present-day football team, is internationally recognized. The Franco regime suppressed the Catalan language but it was only ever off the boil rather than culturally cold and it simmered away for decades before exploding back into parlance. This distinct tongue is the rich linguistic fruit in the multi-layered cake which gives the region its flavour and makes it not so much a part of Spain as a unique outpost of Europe.

The three regions of Catalonia which hold so much promise for the future as well as cutting the mustard today are Penedes itself (which specializes in the increasingly elegant Cava sparkling wines as well as Cabernet Sauvignon, Chardonnay, Merlot, Riesling, Carinena, Sauvignon Blanc, Pinot Noir, Garnacha and Tempranillo, to mention but the best-known varieties), Costers del Segre (of which the Raimat wine company and vineyard management team is the most exciting) and Conca de Barbera (one of Spain's newest demarcated wine areas – that is to say, its producers are entitled to 'so label the provenance of each and every bottle produced within its strictly demarcated borders).

I except from this list the old Catalonian area of Priorato, of which Conca de Barbera is within shouting distance, because although it does produce some exciting, alcoholic and potently fruity reds, these show no evidence of developing any further than they have done already, and though I might personally like to see bottles of Priorato on supermarket and high street wine retailer shelves (only Wine Cellar, the Greenalls chain, has a bottle at the time of writing) these are almost exclusively the reserve of the specialist Spanish wine importer. Priorato can be heady enough to revive a corpse.

It must be recorded, however, that there is something of a contradiction in calling Catalonia a great region of the future, for two of the grape varieties mentioned above, which to give them their French names are Carignan and Grenache, originally came from Catalonia, or were certainly first exported from its ports, over 600 years ago, and ended up in the Rhône Valley where they are widely assumed to be native varieties. It must also be said that Catalonians were cultivating vines at least three or four centuries before those great vine colonizers the ancient Romans arrived around 200 BC. So to label the region as a future star when it has such a well-established vinous history is a bit of a cheek. But then it is true to say that the region was in the doldrums by the early twentieth century and the wine-makers demoralized, vine diseases having devastated the crops.

PENEDES

Penedes only re-established itself as a newly galvanized force to be reckoned with by wine critics in 1979 – right around the time that English revolutionary Mrs Margaret Thatcher was first getting herself elected. In that year, almost two decades after Miguel Torres first introduced to Spain such modern techniques as stainless-steel fermentation tanks for white wine, a Torres bottle, **Gran Coronas Black Label Cabernet Sauvignon 1970** from the Mas La Plana vineyard trounced the greatest Cabernets of France, some of which were classic vintages (like **Chateau Latour 1970**), in a so-called Wine Olympics. A 1971 vintage of the same wine (though this vintage also contained small percentages of Tempranillo and Cabernet Franc and so was not a 100 per cent Cabernet Sauvignon) repeated its triumph against Bordeaux reds in 1990 when it was anonymously entered in a similar wine-tasting challenge. It triumphed over everything including Lafite and Mouton Rothschild (not surprisingly, I would have said, but then I suspect I'm in a minority in regarding these latter wines as overrated and underfruited).

These absurd events – absurd because wine is not intended to be evaluated alongside other bottles in a cold tasting room but is designed to be relished with food in a warm dining room – created a famous wine, a fabled wine-maker, and a legendary wine region. This is why Torres wines, irrespective of their merits, feature on so many French restaurants' wine lists in France when you might have thought foreign wines anathema.

I have never tasted the 1970 vintage of the Gran Coronas Black Label but I once enjoyed a bottle of the '83 (in 1993) with Catalan food and it was an exciting meal. The 1988 vintage of this wine, which is rich but will in my view develop more expressively in bottle in a few years' time, is available at Oddbins for almost £20, and other stockists have included Laymont and Shaw, wine merchants of Truro in Cornwall who specialize in Spain, and Tanners Wines of Shrewsbury. There are various vintages of **Mas La Plana** available at various small wine merchants, and the odd restaurant, around the country: the '71, the '76, the '77, the '78, the '83, and the '85 (which is everywhere from the Ritz Hotel and Le Gavroche in London to a whole posse of stickleback-sized merchants who make up for what they lack in size in enthusiasm for the wine). If you are interested in tracking this wine down, then the person to contact is Ms Alison Dillon at John E. Fells & Sons, trade wine merchant of Birkbeck Grove London W3 (tel.: 0181 749 3661), who will tell you where to go.

COSTERS DEL SEGRE

Following on from this Torres upstart from Penedes – an area which was already beginning to make a name for itself with sparkling wine enthusiasts – a new region called Costers del Segre got into the act. Now this region owes its origins to the sheer unadulterated *chutzpah* of a crafty devil called Don

Manuel Raventos Domenech. Don Manuel purchased a desert and turned it into a grape garden of Eden. He acquired his plot of seemingly worthless soil, some 8000 acres of it, near the town of Lerida, in 1914, when so saline was the terrain that nothing would grow. What Don Manuel knew was that the imminent construction of the Catalonia and Aragon canal would ensure the flow of beautiful water fresh from the Pyrenees through his property and this would be instrumental in turning a wasteland into a fecund landscape. The water dissipated the salt, helped by the planting and subsequent sacrifice of trees which prepared the soil in readiness for the future vines. This took thirty years to be fully achieved and the real fruit of this great vision has only been reaped in recent years when the wine produced on the estate has proved so outstanding that it has been responsible for the elevation of the Costers del Segre area to Denominacion Internacional (DO) status. That is to say, it is now a Region of Origin with strictly demarcated borders and a code of quality.

The name of the wine company and vineyard operation responsible for this is Raimat, a wholly owned subsidiary of the well-known Codorniu Cava house of which Don Manuel was the big cheese. (He was always a clever clogs. He was born to it. His father created Cava in 1872, having lifted the idea from the Champagne region. And Don Manuel himself, before he used his Cava profits to buy all that desert, had introduced many public relations and advertising techniques, some of which the wiliest practitioner in today's publicity industry would be hard put to match for originality and panache.) The winery building which now abuts the vineyards is one of the most beautifully designed in Spain, carrying on the great tradition of Catalan flair for architecture and design.

The Raimat company, growing classic grape varieties like Merlot, Tempranillo, Cabernet Sauvignon and Chardonnay, makes outstanding wines at prices around a fiver. These are, or certainly have been, on sale at all the leading wine shops and supermarkets but have never quite taken off in the way that they deserve (though there was a minor technical problem once when certain barrels caused some of the wines to be rather unpleasantly woody and coarse).

My favourite Raimat wine is the special blend which Marks and Spencer caused to be specially put together for them. This is called **Gran Calesa 1990** and it is a stunning get-together of Merlot, Tempranillo and Cabernet Sauvignon. It is an absolutely fabulous wine for under a fiver. The fruit is almost magically rich and softly textured with a finish of vivacity and such flourish that the drinker cannot help but insist on further glasses simply to check whether his senses have not been deceiving him. Early in January 1996, M&S took delivery of the 1991 vintage. Vintages, like the directional skills of Grand National jockeys and the good sense of one's children, cannot ever be taken for granted, and I had hoped it might be even deeper than the '90. But, for the time being at least, this is not to be. It is still a decent wine but less immediately gripping than its predecessor. However, it will, I believe, age gracefully and concentrate its fruitiness and become, within a few years, a wine of class with a lush velvet texture.

It is a great pity that someone of Don Manuel's flair and energy is not responsible for making Raimat better known in the UK in the 1990s. Were such an individual to be so briefed, armed with such a bunch of terrific wines in his carpetbag, Raimat would be on everyone's lips, in restaurant, wine bar and around the dinner table

CONCA DE BARBERA

The third area of Catalonia which I believe has a great future is Conca de Barbera. This is a very new area and only achieved DO status in 1989, one year after Costers del Segre. Miguel Torres has a vineyard here, which until recently produced the most renowned wine of the area (not that anyone was aware of the fact from the label for it never claimed Conca de Barbera status, preferring to state simply that it came from Penedes). This is a Chardonnay called Milmanda and the 1993 of this wine, costing around £15, is to be had at small wine merchants only (Direct Wine Shipments of Belfast, King and Barnes of Horsham, and London Wine in SW10). This is a very beautiful Chardonnay indeed of classic weight of structure and extremely elegant fruit. It stands comparison with the finest of its kind from the Hunter Valley in Australia, the Napa Valley in California, and Marlborough in New Zealand. Stick-in-the-muds may also claim that certain rare and wonderful white burgundies are up to being compared with it, but the only experience I have to support this contention is a single bottle of very young and very famous Meursault which cost £25. Having said that, I would unquestionably rate Milmanda more delicious and more delicately sensual (which is the benchmark of great Chardonnay) than all other white burgundies I have tasted in the last decade, including obscenely expensive bottles of Corton-Charlemagne costing a postman's weekly wage.

Yet it is not for this wine that Conca de Barbera merits our attention. Milmanda, hiding its origins, always seemed a freak – like an English tennis player reaching the Wimbledon final. But the flood of superb red wines which has rolled down the Conca's steep slopes (for the area is the highest in Catalonia) has demonstrated that high-growing vines, with the advantage of cool nights to encourage the build-up of acids to counterbalance the fruit sugars which proliferate through the abundance of an often ferocious day-time sun, are equally good at producing red wines as white.

Over the past three years the Barberans must have felt like a royal prince contemplating nuptials or like one of those oriental mystics to whose door (or more likely doormat) the questioning world beats a path. The flying wine-makers have flown in and out, the supermarket and high street wine chain wine buyers have come knocking with their pockets stuffed with ready dosh, and the likes of me, the parasitic wine hack who is always the last to hear of anything, has arrived primed with a pen full of ready ink as the actual wines themselves, all under four quid and some well under, have sloshed deliciously over his taste-buds: **Fuente del Ritmo** (Oddbins), **Conca de Barbera** (Marks and Spencer), **Santara Cabernet Merlot** (just about everybody, it seems), **Tierra Seca** (Oddbins), **Castillo de Mont Blanc** (last seen at Fullers wine shops).

Hugh Ryman, the ubiquitous Englishman who makes wine everywhere but Antarctica (but give him time) and Ed Flaherty (an Irish/Cuban Californian who made his name in Chile) are the most active foreign influences in the region.

Travelling oenologists are encouraged to operate here because wine co-operatives exist; there are very few grape-growers who actually make their own wine. The amount of international press attention given to flying wine-makers has made them the darling of the boondocks wine co-op looking to jazz up its range, introduce new technology and revitalize its member growers' viticultural practices and, as a consequence, find favour with that most treasured of wine buyers: the man or woman from the British retailer. The actual climate of the Spanish wine industry as a whole, and the internal decline of sales over the past ten years as a new generation of drinkers have turned off wine and looked to beer and other drinks, has forced many wine producers to consider offshore markets which they may never have seriously contemplated before.

COTES DU ROUSSILLON

I have been increasingly excited about various red wines from the Languedoc-Roussillon region as a whole for a dozen or more years. And, in the last three years, more and more white wines have appeared, in particular Chardonnays and Sauvignon Blancs, which are impressive, varietally precise, and very inexpensive. However, it is the Roussillon part of the

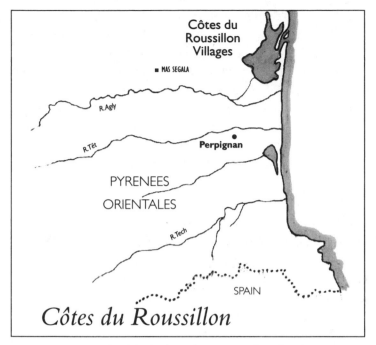

Côtes du
Roussillon
Villages

■ MAS SEGALA

R.Agly

R.Têt

Perpignan

PYRENEES
ORIENTALES

R.Tech

SPAIN

Côtes du Roussillon

region I want to highlight here because it has dazzling potential – a potential which, in wine like **Mas Segala Cotes du
Roussillon Villages 1993** and **1994**, it has already realized.

The Roussillon is Catalan France, in fact: it borders the
Pyrenees and Spain. It has the driest climate in France and,
more often than not, the warmest. Its best wines are red, made
from Syrah, Carignan and Grenache grapes. The vintages have
been consistently good: '95, '94, '93 and '91. It is a clue as to
how good the grapes grown here are that the region also
produces superb cherries, peaches and apricots. It is a region
stamped in mystique and as recently as the 1930s there were
British travel writers who had never penetrated it, in the
belief that it still harboured medieval sorcerers who drank
foreigners' blood. The wines – and food – of the region were
despised. ('In food the taste of the Roussillonnais is coarse.
His wine, in the condition in which he drinks it, is thick and
heady. The addiction in a hot climate to a diet of pork …
supplemented on feast days by vast quantities of snails is hard–

ly evidence of refinement.' Basil Collier, *Catalan France*, 1939.)

The region as a whole was granted AOC status, that is to say, entitled to put Appellation Cotes du Roussillon Contrôlée or Appellation Cotes du Roussillon Villages Contrôlée on its labels, only in 1977. It seems ironic, to me at least, that a region from where so many Bordeaux and Burgundy wine merchants in days gone by bought wine to add some sunshine to their own pitifully inadequate wines should today stand on the threshold of being one of the next century's most exciting wine areas.

Wines – good deep reds, like **Domaine de la Figarede**, **Chateau Saint Pierre** and the straightforward **Cotes du Roussillon**, all made by one of France's most important, most vital, most innovative (yet never entirely tradition-rejecting) co-operatives called Les Vignerons du Val d'Orbieu – have shown themselves as fine bargains in the past. This co-op is huge and active throughout the Languedoc-Roussillon area. The Vignerons Catalan co-op also turns out some excellent three-quid reds. Some of these wines do not receive AOC status. They can be labelled Vin de Pays des Pyrenees-Orientales.

> ▶ **Wines to look out for**
> Chateau de Corneilla
> Domaine Bousquet-Cornelade
> Domaine Cazes * * * – but expensive
> Domaine Vignon
> Domaine de Rombeau
> Chateau Lasfous
> Chateau Planeres
> Domaine Pierre Picquemal
> Chateau de Jau
> Domaine Muillet de Broca
> Domaine Gauby
> Caramany
> Domaine Saint Martin
> Chateau de Blanes
> Cullens and Amberley

The loveliest white wine of the region, the rich, honeyed **Rivesaltes**, which is widely available at wine shops, is probably not hugely different in style from that so admired all those years ago by Pliny the Elder. Indeed, in producing sweet wines Roussillon made a unique contribution to wine-making techniques. This was the discovery, in the late thirteenth century, that adding alcohol to fermenting must stops the ferment, thus permitting much residual sugar to be retained. These wines are referred to as *vins licoreux*.

I have enjoyed many of the basic Cotes du Roussillon rouges over the past few years but none came close to being such a fruity bargain as Somerfield's, labelled nothing fancier than Cotes du Roussillon. It was, in May 1995, £1.99 a bottle, and soft, earthy, eminently gluggable stuff it was, although, needless to say, it found little favour with the stuck-up wine critics who despised its positive fruit and its puny price. However, if there is one wine from the Cotes du Roussillon I admire above all others, it is the Mas Segala referred to earlier. The Mas Segala vineyard, which in 1987 was just ten acres and now stretches to seventy-five, is owned by Sylvie and Charles Faisant. Monsieur Faisant works for another winery altogether, Les Vignerons Foncalieu, based near Carcassonne, where he is sales manager. He grows Grenache, Carignan and Syrah, and if any wine in Roussillon demonstrates the vast and exciting potential for such fruit, grown on good slatey soil, it is Mas Segala. Asda is most keen on this wine, stocking the '93 and '94 in the past, and both vintages were excellent. At less than £4 a bottle, Mas Segala is a logan-, black- and raspberry-flavoured bargain, a wine of real character, soft texture and delicious violet-scented fruit. It is dark and dry and had sufficient wood and fruit tannins to last and develop well in bottle for two to three years more.

When M. Faisant began making wine at Mas Segala it was just a part-time interest. But what now? Doubtless he will wait for future developments to occur in their own good time. After all, Roussillon has a history of being innovative ahead of everyone else while keeping itself to itself.

Were not the remains of the first officially accredited European human being first unearthed in the Tantavel area of Roussillon, precisely where Mas Segala is situated? The old boy was half-a-million years old. I hope we don't have to wait as long before Mas Segala is turning out enough good wine to be on more wine shop shelves.

7

DON'T GET SCREWED, GET SCREWCAPPED

'If the cork smells of cork, it's bad; the cork should smell of the wine … and a wine that tastes of cork is no good. Send it back and ask for another bottle, just as you would if you were served a bad egg.' Alexis Lichine,
The Wines of France, 1952

There is an exquisite torture involved in buying wine which recalls the arctic British winters of years ago, before the electronic starter motor was invented, when families would clamber aboard the old Austin and in their hearts would fester the dread that this would be one of those times when the starting handle would be unable to budge the ice-cold engine and another trip would be ruined before it even began. Every time I uncork a bottle of wine, I feel the same cold dread until I've smelt the cork and then the wine and I know that it will start smoothly. I feel this especially when it isn't a bottle sent to me by a retailer to sample but one I've paid good money for, either in a shop or a restaurant, because if it is duff then I've got to negotiate a fresh bottle or ask for a refund.

It's easier in a restaurant because I can simply send the criminal wine back and get a new one. Yet even here I sometimes feel embarrassed about the procedure. Like the time I sent back the first bottle on three separate visits to a new hotspot, called The Sugar Club, which opened up locally to my home. When it happened the third time I really felt like a heel. But the wine was corked each time, dammit, so why was I feeling bad about it? Why did I not feel free instantly to seek recompense or replacement? The restaurant manager was perfectly charming about it all and had no trouble agreeing with my assessment when he tasted the offending bottle side by side with the second and perfect one. Yet I'm supposed to be a pro. So if I feel uncomfortable about this sort of thing — not least because I hate the thought that my companions might think I'm just showing off as certain ignorant brutes are rumoured to do regularly as a matter of course with the first bottle they receive — how might less experienced and knowledgeable folk feel?

Corked wine is undoubtedly nothing new. What is new is the incidence of its discovery. I believe our ancestors — recently, not just in the 1950s or before the war, let alone in the last century — regularly drank wine which was corked. In those days the great wines, indeed all wines, were exclusively the province of the toff or the successful professional and they were invariably old. It is only with contemporary advent of New World wines, especially Australian, Californian, New Zealand, South African, Chilean and so forth, that the problem has been seen to be so pernicious, so widespread, so damaging. This is because far more wines are made nowadays, and more corks produced, and most of these wines are meant to be drunk young. The freshness and vibrancy of their fruit are one of their most attractive features and the merest degree of cork taint mars the wines measurably. The EC working commission looking into the problems of the cork industry in Portugal estimates that cork-tainted wines cost Europe several hundred million pounds a year.

Wine, it is now admitted, is many times dud — all because of the cork. Yet many a normal drinker feels alienated in the course of bringing this to the

> ❛ Wine, it is now admitted, is many times dud — all because of the cork. Yet many a normal drinker feels alienated in bringing this to the attention of the powers that be. ❜

attention of the powers that be. Contrast this alienation with the scenario below, which occurred for real, in May 1995, while I was idling in a bookshop.

NOT A COMPLETE CHANGE OF CLIMATE
A TWO-MINUTE PLAY INVOLVING A CUSTOMER, A SHOP
ASSISTANT AND AN ON-LOOKER

Scene: The cash-till area of a busy modern book store. A dozen or more customers bustle about looking vaguely preoccupied or literary. A young male assistant is absorbed with some papers he is studying behind the counter. Close by, a wine writer, easily identified by his ruby cheeks and habit of smelling each book as he picks it up, idly rummages through a pile of newly published thrillers. The large glass doors opening on to the street burst open and an agitated young woman rushes up to the young man at the counter. She is slightly out of breath. She waves a paperback book under the man's nose and gesticulates.

Woman: Look! I bought this book and…(pant pant)… I get to this page… (pant)… almost at the end … and look! … no more words. Only blank pages where the words should be.

Man: Well, I've never seen that before.

Woman: Me neither. I jumped off the number 12 bus I was so irritated…

Man: Well, let me get you a new one right away. Or do you want your money back?

Woman: Oh no! I must have a new copy. I must finish it. It's so wonderfully written.

Man (holds up the book and we see that it is a Penguin paperback called A Change of Climate *by Hilary Mantel):* I agree! You must have felt livid when you discovered these blank pages....

Wine writer (who has been captivated by this exchange, not only because he has inordinate admiration for Hilary Mantel's book and understands perfectly how the customer must feel but because he has found much to ponder over in the incident and furiously begins to write in his notebook): ...Cough.

Woman: Yes! I could hardly believe it. But I must tell you that I didn't buy it at this branch. I bought it in your Charing Cross Road one ...

Man: No matter. You must have a new book. I'll go and get one for you.

Wine writer (thinking to himself and scribbling): How less confident this customer would feel if she had bought a dud bottle instead of a duff book. And how different would be the reception she would get if she summoned up the nerve to return it to the shop she bought it from.

END

What a civilized exchange unfolds above. But what is significant about it, for our purposes, is not the pleasantness of the assistant but the confidence of the customer. She never doubted for a minute that she should act as she did. Who in her right mind would accept as perfectly normal the idea that now and then books will fail to finish because of printing gaffes? Yet too many wines fail to please, because they do not finish or even start as they should, thereby

> ❛ Why should we meekly accept faults in wine, almost exclusively but not entirely caused by contaminated corks, that we do not for one second tolerate in other products? ❜

disappointing their purchasers, yet few people take them for exchange or a refund. Why should we meekly accept faults in wine, almost exclusively but not entirely caused by contaminated corks, that we do not for one second tolerate in other products?

One reason for accepting faulty wine is that few people spot it as such, unless the fault is so horrendously obvious that the wine is disgusting and undrinkable. But this does not happen very often. Most faults merely rob the wine of its bloom, the freshness of its fruit, the pertness of its acidity or, with older wines, the depth and majesty of its flavour. These faults are subtle. An edge has been removed, that is all. Many so-called experts fail to see these faults, so the normal customer is even less likely to recognize them as such (they will merely experience less pleasure about something over which they feel, erroneously, they have no control).

Viognier Vin de Pays d'Oc (£4.99) which I was given to sample at a wine-tasting organized by Waitrose last year was tasted by two Masters of Wine employed by the store and not one of them spotted it was corked until this was pointed out. Likewise, the Californian wine-maker (the man who actually *made* the wine no less!) who refused to accept the verdict of wine buyer Steve Daniel of Oddbins when Steve said his wine was corked went so far as to expostulate that the wine was perfect the way it tasted. Steve refused to accept this and submitted samples for laboratory analysis. Back came the scientific proof: the wine was minutely polluted with cork taint.

But the most resonant reason for our tolerance of duff wine is our feeling of being out of our depth if we complain about it. And so we're back with that familiar theme which pops up like a wicked witch's curse throughout this book. This curse insinuates that appreciation of wine is a specialized gift and ordinary joes should keep their traps shut about it, closet their thoughts inside their ignorant heads, and accept the odd bottle of unsatisfactory wine as just one of life's insoluble mysteries (which all adds to the romantic mystique of wine and allows the so-called connoisseur to retain his status).

The ritual of the cork is, as dozens of middle-aged male wine merchants the length and breadth of Britain have dynamically confirmed to me when I broached the subject, part of the romance of wine. The rites of passage of every male wine-drinker involve, at one time or another (and with some hairy-bottomed brutes all the time), the woman passing him the corkscrew (much as she would, 500 years ago, have blessed his lance prior to a joust) and whispering slavishly, 'Do the honours, will you, darling?' And in goes that spiral of steel, the man heaves and grunts (often with the bottle between his thighs), and out comes the cork. Triumph! He has slain the villainous black knight.

But of course the real villain of the piece is that inch and a bit of cork so smugly impaled on the end of the corkscrew. Is it a perfect, taint-free cork? Or is it, however mildly, a bad 'un? Will our white knight smell the end of the cork and, knowing what to look for if he finds a whiff of something suspicious, open another bottle?

No, he will not. He might smell the cork and detect, not the aroma of wine, but a faint mustiness or mushroomy smell. The smell might be a touch cardboardy or of rotten wood. But isn't a cork supposed to smell of this? If the wine is red, and of some years' age, and if it has been barrel-fermented and/or aged, won't there be the smell of wood? Isn't it natural that a wine like this should have woody odours on its cork? The answer is yes, but only to a certain extent. If the cork is a pure, neutral stopper as it is *intended* to be, then what you should smell is the wine – nothing else. The wine itself, red or white, may be woody and so naturally this is part of the effect its maker intends. It may be overwoody, but this may be oenological cackhandedness, not the sign of a faulty cork. You see how tricky and how fraught with subtle thorns this field of enquiry is?

Yet I believe that anyone who finds a wine less fruity, fresh or vivid than it should be, or than he or she has been led to expect, should complain, because that wine, however mildly, is corked. Send it packing! It is a fact that the only reason corked wines continue to exist is because we DON'T complain enough.

If, every time a restaurant wine or retailer-bought bottle which failed to please because it didn't taste right was returned whence it came, either for replacement or refund, corked, faulty wines would have disappeared years ago. There is so little pressure placed on restaurants and retailers by their customers that these purveyors of wine place no pressure on their suppliers in turn and so the problem is deemed not worth solving.

I cannot tell you how violently I reject the idea that we must put up with corked wines and corkscrews. The tolerance of both is as absurd as if the modern car with all its incredible technological wizardry was still dependent upon the starting handle. I would like to banish corks and corkscrews to a museum for future generations to hoot at in derision. I am attached to the notion that wine is simply an everyday enjoyment, not a subject for fanciful 'expert' preaching, and corks falsely muddy that notion and give it a layer of unnatural depth which helps to maintain the subject of wine as an arcane, specialized subject.

Yet the answer to the problem of corked wine is simple. Every wine-maker in the world knows it and would like to be the one to offer the solution to his customers. But wine-makers are uniformly a gutless lot who simply won't seize the chance to solve the problem once and for all. In spite of knowing that between 5 and 10 per cent of their wines will not taste as they should when opened by their ultimate consumers, wine-makers hesitate to take the resolute, final

> ❛ I am attached to the notion that wine is simply an everyday enjoyment, not a subject for fanciful 'expert' preaching... ❜

and utterly foolproof step which will end corked wine at a stroke (or, I should say, a twist).

The answer is to use screwcaps. The cork should be given the elbow and this guaranteed faultless seal used instead. Indeed, I had thought, until last Christmas, that all my nagging and complaining about corks and my preference for screwcaps had finally paid off. One of Australia's leading wine companies, BRL Hardy, agreed with me and said, 'Okay, let's seal a couple of our finest wines, Chateau Reynella Basket-Press Shiraz and Chardonnay, with screwcaps.' The UK representatives of the company were ecstatic at the idea. I was over the moon. We both knew of the results of the side-by-side trials when the same wines were screwcapped and corked – assembled panels of wine experts were unable to tell the difference between the two (except when one of the cork-sealed wines was tainted). I had thought I was on the threshold of the second revolution involving screwcaps. Are you old enough to remember the fuss that was made when spirit producers dumped corks, many decades ago now, and went over to screwcaps? Does anyone today look down on a screw-capped bottle of whisky or brandy as inferior because it is so sealed?

BRL Hardy recognized, as do I, that although certain litre bottles of cheap French wine have been screwcapped in the past, and still are, there is a degree of perceived second-rateness about such a method of sealing. I applauded the company's bravery in leaping this possible stumbling-block to the plan. Some years ago another Australian wine company tried out screwcaps on the home market for one of its wines and the result was a disaster. The wine was fine, the screwcaps kept it as fresh as it should have been, but the poor bottle was regarded as a container of second-rate wine. Customers hated the idea. They scorned to buy the wine. It was, then, going to take a courageous Aussie to fly in the face of this previous fiasco and screwcap a wine – especially a wonderful wine with a recognized following in Australia and in export markets like the UK.

However, just as the button to set the screwcapping machinery in motion was about to be pressed, an inventor appeared on BRL Hardy's doorstep with a remarkable substance. It was an elastomeric alloy which, unlike the plastic corks which Marks and Spencer has been pioneering in up to twenty of its wines over the past five years, and the bright yellow plastic cork Penfolds use for a Semillon they sell to Safeway, is capable of being manufactured to varying degrees of elasticity. Incredibly, the stuff derives from the substance which is used in Australia to make bumper bars on cars. And its variable elasticity means that it answers one of the unsolved riddles of the plastic cork – how will it perform in a wine made to age for twenty or more years?

There is evidence, though I must confess it was news to me, that wines made to age for donkey's years acquire some character through the entrance of an incredibly tiny amount of air, via the cork, into the wine. The amount gaining admittance must be so minute as to be barely calculable but, nevertheless, if this is true (which, personally, I do not fully accept), then any sealant for such a wine would need to be sufficiently porous to permit this aeration in microscopic amounts yet equally robust to withstand years in a cellar. The new elastomeric alloy, because it can be manufactured in different elastic strengths with degrees of porosity, can therefore be used to make synthetic corks for all wines: wines to drink within a year or two of being made as well as the fancy growths of Bordeaux and elsewhere which are designed to lie on their sides and develop for decades. Further, this alloy looks like a cork, takes a corkscrew like a cork, will never pass on any taint to the wine, being an utterly neutral seal, and is cheaper than cork. Anthony Smith, the managing director of the South Australian company responsible for marketing this idea (which is, in fact, a leading natural cork processing business selling corks to hundreds of wineries), told me, when he telephoned me with news of the development, that 'the average consumer will think it's cork. It's identical to a composite cork.'

In the face of intervention by this hopefully miracle recipe, my scheme to see **Chateau Reynella**, one of the best wines in this book, topped by a metal screw-offable cap collapsed in ruins. I may scorn the men at BRL Hardy for their last-minute reversion to type (i.e. men and the blasted corkscrew ritual) but, if the trials with the alloy are successful – and since these are taking place as this book goes to press I cannot report on them here – then at least I can rejoice that the consumers of good wine will never have to take a bottle back on the grounds that it was corked.

In one way, I should shun the idea of plastic corks or elastomeric alloy corks altogether. They are, of course, still corks. And corks require corkscrews. Am I the only wine drinker in the world who would like never again to have to struggle with a corkscrew? When the cork industry in Portugal, a frag-mented operation with many quality-

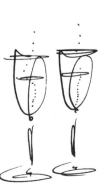

control problems (spread over thousands of cork tree growers and 600 processors of the bark), finally becomes a part of history like those poor boys who crawled up inside Victorian chimneys, I will be happy because corked wines will be a thing of the past as well. But I will not be pleased to see the corkscrew given a reprieve.

▶ **Chateau Reynella Shiraz**, around £7 (available at Fullers, Oddbins and Waitrose). This wine is, as its label announces, 'basket-pressed'. This means that a so-called basket press, which looks like a Heath Robinson marriage between an early Gutenberg printing machine and an old wooden barrel, was used instead of more modern equipment. This is a gentle way of handling grapes, though a modern bladder press, where the grapes are not crushed so much as pressed by a gently expanding airbag inside a rotary drum, might serve the purpose equally well. But the words on the label wouldn't sound so cosy, mystic or reassuringly traditional. Be all this as it may, Chateau Reynella Basket-Press Shiraz is a beautifully textured wine of rich fruit and great class. A deeply stylish bargain at the price — basket or no basket.

Damn you, Anthony Smith and BRL Hardy and all the other Australian wine companies who are interested in the idea (which includes Southcorp, who are the Penfolds people, Yalumba and Mildara–Blass)! These synthetic corks, if they are a success and widely adopted, will keep a ridiculous and irrelevant ritual going. I may happily swallow the contents of bottles sealed with elastomeric alloy corks, but I will never comfortably swallow the idea of the instrument used to remove them. Corkscrews, like the Mensheviks, should be consigned to the dustbin of history and collected, for want of a healthier hobby, by nutters.

▶In April 1996, Christies held an auction of 'the private corkscrew collection of Richard Dennis, expected to realize in excess of £50,000'. Dennis was, Christies reported, a founder member of the ICCA (International Correspondence of Corkscrew Addicts).

▶ IMPORTANT STOP PRESS

As this book was in its final stages, Penfolds telephoned me to say they would like to experiment in the UK with people's reactions to a screwcap on one of its red wines. The wine is Bin 2 South Eastern Australian Shiraz-Mourvedre 1994, a rich, deep red of some class. I was delighted. This is no ordinary glug, Bin 2. It's drinkable now, with its spicy, dry but firmly fruity style and warmly textured fruit, but it will develop in bottle for several years to come and soften, I suspect, most impressively. This wine costs around £5.50 at Victoria Wine, Thresher, Oddbins, Majestic Wine Warehouses, Wine Cellar and Fullers amongst wine shop chains, and it's in Waitrose and Sainsbury's supermarkets.

Best of all – all you have to do to unleash its fruit is twist off the cap. And not a single bottle will suffer from cork taint.

8 | The Thirteen Biggest Whoppers In Wine

'...I wanted to cook up a sumptuous repast of roast loin of pork, wild rice wrapped in banana leaves, and pencil-thin asparagus, capped off with a bottle of La Tache 1947... I passed an afternoon judging its "bouquet" and "body" and ... fell asleep on the davenport ... the empty bottle ... on the coffee table beside me.'
Frederick Exley, A Fan's Notes, 1970

There are many false ideas about wine. Some have grown up by accident, others have been deliberately created. A good few became Great Lies by being fostered by those with a vested interest in so doing, others lie around like sleeping alligators with the truth of their toothless gums and benign dispositions never revealed. There are, of course, a good deal more than a comfortable round or baker's dozen of these pernicious untruths. But a dozen makes a bargain case (with one bottle thrown in free) — and a full case of wine lies seemed too obvious, and too entertaining, a parcel to ignore.

Lie 1: Wine is a difficult subject which only a few gifted individuals know anything about and can write about

This is a Great Lie, fostered by wine writers and critics, wine sales-persons and publicists (and not a few wine marketeers), many of whom dare openly to call themselves experts. But in reality most of them are merely well practised. The everyday drinker knows something about wine of which the so-called wine buff or wine critic has not the remotest inkling. And this is what he or she likes to drink. How many wine experts, even those who have readers for whom they write, know what drinkers like? Well, I will tell them. Most readers like fruit. They don't like spending a lot of money very often either and when they do (say over a tenner but no more than £15), they want something glorious and as fantastic as a royal grandstand seat at the Cup Final of the century.

Critics are mostly a self-obsessed species. Indeed, their absorption in their subject is the only thing which prevents many of them from becoming total solipsists. Certainly, for some critics, their subject is a veneer which, however superficial, protects them from teetering over the edge into complete madness. The mistake is to imagine that such critics care about their readers and thus take their readers' interests even remotely into account. Like film critics or theatre critics or even food critics (with the notable exceptions of late luminaries like James Agee, Kenneth Tynan or Elizabeth David amongst several others), the subject under review is an expression of the writer's own mind and inclinations, and the only thing being addressed is a mirror.

Personally, I despise this approach. I have enjoyed glorious evenings in the theatre, at the cinema, and in restaurants all of which were damned by the critics, and I have endured the very opposite of enjoyable evenings at such places when the critics have been wildly approving.

Critics may be, and of necessity cannot help but be, true to themselves as individuals, but what about the audience at which their criticisms are directed? I regard my own readers as a lighthouse of which I lose sight at my peril. I cannot drink any wine without considering what it represents as an object of value for money (or not) and this, as far as I am concerned, legitimizes what I do. I am my readers' palate, liver and stomach. My readers give me my living. I do my utmost to give them terrific value-for-money wines. It is a two-way relationship.

To be sure, I have my own preferences for certain wines but equally I do not find it irksome or difficult to put myself in the place of a readership which may have a partiality for wines of an utterly different temper. This requires an act of the imagination of a different order than the creativity required of a writer. It is, however, an act of the imagination beyond almost all but a few writers on wine – as is, for that matter, any creativity worth the name. Judgements on wine made by partners, or teams, or, worst of all, committees, are worthless. Only individuals pass any opinions on wine worth considering.

> 6 I am my readers' palate, liver and stomach. My readers give me my living. I do my utmost to give them terrific value-for-money wines. 9

The individual wine writer, however, is valuable only in as far as you can judge that his or her palate matches your own and therefore is likely to feel the same way as you might do about the same wines. So far so good. But there is still the problem of the circumstances in which the wine was judged and there is still a vital question to be asked of the writer who writes about it. The circumstances, which are often the artificial ones of a structured wine-tasting, do not lend themselves to a proper appreciation of wine except by the most disciplined of minds. Judgements as to whether or not a wine is value for money are completely outside many wine writers' expertise and most certainly their personal viewpoint. And as to the other vital question, which is concerned with how the wine might perform with food and what sort this might be, it is often totally ignored.

What social purpose, then, does the wine writer serve if he or she cannot tell his or her readers whether a wine is worth the money or what food it might go with? I am entirely of the opinion that the huge reputation of Australian wines in this country is almost exclusively due to wine writers assessing them favourably in wine-tastings when many of the wines, were they to be considered in partnership with food, would not be so highly regarded. The artificial nature of the formal wine-tasting is entirely responsible for this. The number of wine critics who can consistently produce useful judgments about such wines and how they will perform with food is calculable on the fingers of one hand. Add to this a widespread inability to provide value-for-money judgements and you have what in other professional circles would be regarded as a professional crisis. But then wine writing is not a profession because so few of its practitioners are professional. (Although the stunningly accurate observation George Bernard Shaw passed on this subject, to wit: 'All professions are conspiracies against the laity', perfectly applies here.)

If it wasn't for the seductive notion attached to wine – a notion which used to be confined to the Western world but has now spread to the Pacific Rim and Japan – which elevates expertise in the subject to something remarkable which only a few gifted souls can understand, wine writers would be as redundant as filing clerks. I sometimes feel embarrassed to tell sensibly employed souls that I am a wine writer. What a ridiculous thing to be! I might with more pride describe myself as an equine dentist, and I only feel justified in pursuing this risible avenue of employment because of the encouragement I receive from readers and the view they seem to take that I am a help in finding them bargains. I sleep soundly knowing my readers are drinking sensibly and, I hope, healthily. But call me a wine expert? No, thank you. Label me a wine buff? Ugh! Suggest I am a wine snob! I'll sue!!

I am a wine enthusiast. And all I do is pass that enthusiasm on. (Old George Bernard also remarked that 'Happy is the man who can make his hobby his profession' and I entirely concur.)

Lie 2: *Cheap German wine is sweet and nasty and peppered with sulphur and the good stuff costs an arm and a leg (and smells horribly of petrol anyway)*

I will not ennoble this absurd prejudice, which in many respects is wildly out of date, with a detailed response. I will refute it with a single bottle: **Ruppertsberger Hofstuck**

Riesling Kabinett 1993 (Asda, £2.99). This not only represents amazing value (for it will age and develop the so-called
'petrolly' undertones which are not remotely offensive but are
in fact deliciously aromatic and complex) but stands for a new
direction for the classic Rhine wine style, or hock as it was
called by our forefathers. The Ruppertsberg wine co-op is a
superbly run establishment, doing things in a very modern way
yet still retaining a deep respect for certain of the traditional
customs, and this wine is not sweet but then neither is it
off-puttingly arid and dry. It is whistle-clean and subtle, with a
beautiful texture to the fruit as if sheen and polish were edible
constructs (and not just a wine writer's fancy). It is a stunning
aperitif wine, but with a few more years under its belt, it will
accompany smoked fish superbly. The last few years' vintages
have all been excellent (and aged well), so the '94, which may
well be available as this book hits the shelves, will, I hope,
maintain the high quality of the fruit and continue to promote
equally high standards of vinification.

I must also commend the giant St Ursula wine co-op in
the Rheinpfalz for its Devil's Rock Riesling 1994 (approxi-
mately £3.50 at Asda, Co-op, Morrison, Tesco and Waitrose).

LIE 3: Soil and climate have the greatest influence on the finished wine

This is a cheeky misconception based on the French genius
for marketing the products of their agricultural labours. Think
about it: if you made something which had to begin life from
the fruit of a plant, and thus was at the mercy of varying
climatic whims as well as the moods of humankind, wouldn't
it be an excellent wheeze to enshrine the uniqueness of your
product by making its very existence inseparable from its
provenance? In the art of wine, the French lead the world (as
once they did in Art with a big A and still do in fragrance
manufacture). But with ham we have Parma, with salmon we
have Scotland, with chocolate we have Switzerland; and these
are all dubious liaisons also, for many regions of the world

produce superb ham (the Spanish *jamon de serrano* is the equal of Parma's any day), New Zealand salmon is richer and more deeply flavoursome than any Scots fish, and the French themselves produce better chocolate than the Swiss.

But with wine, and specifically with the French attitude to it, there has grown up the idea of *terroir*. This has no precise, short English translation. *Terroir* refers to the soil and the meso-climate affecting a single vine-yard site. Straightaway you can see the cunning genius of this notion. It is like the idea behind a custom-built motor car, or an architect-designed maisonette, or a bespoke suit. It confers utter originality and individuality which *cannot be bettered or copied anywhere else*. But it is largely bunkum.

The single most important factor affecting a wine is the person or persons who make it. Of course, such persons cannot do better than the vineyard conditions permit and they cannot make a silken vinous purse from a sow's ear of a grape variety which has suffered from horribly unseasonal weather conditions and a failure to ripen properly. But the influence of the wine-maker is more crucial in the normal course of events than any of these things. Everything that a wine-maker is forced to do, or wishes to do, between the gathering of the grapes to the final bottling of the wine affects the quality, the style, the sheer effect of the wine on the drinker's palate. No matter how advantageous your vineyard, no matter how magnificent your grapes, no matter how clement the season — if you fail to exploit all these benefits then the wine will not be as exciting as it could be, and if you are downright incompetent, greedy or lazy then your wine will be as second-rate as if it were grown in a vineyard a thousand miles away from different grapes through a growing season of uncommon severity.

The La Tache which Frederick Exley (quoted at the beginning of this chapter) researched so exhaustively is one of France's greatest wines. It is a red burgundy from one tiny vineyard exclusively under the control of a single wine-maker which Anthony Hanson, in his book *Burgundy*, says is rarely other than spectacular and fascinating. The other burgundies which merit such effusive praise are not legion, whatever their name.

> **' The single most important factor affecting a wine is the person or persons who make it. '**

Yet every time that I enter a wine shop, or poke about in a branch of a high street wine retailer, and even when I nose about a supermarket's wine shelves, I always come across the odd customer, sometimes whole groups of misguided folk, flying in the face of reason and buying a bottle or bottles of wine purely on the basis of their belief that the words on the label which refer to a vineyard area or a regional *Appellation* mean that they are making a superior choice. These words are just part of the packaging. Much of the time, they have no bearing on the quality of the wine in the bottle in any way, shape or form.

So don't buy wine like the chap I once fell into conversation with at my local supermarket who said to me, 'I think spending fifteen pounds on a bottle with a name like Pommard on the label means I'm going to be pouring out a terrific glass of wine.' No amount of cajoling from me, even to the extent of offering to buy him a bottle, could convince him that he would be better off spending £2.99 on a bottle of Romanian Pinot Noir – especially since the rich meaty meal he said he was aiming to partner the wine with would crush the Pommard but only bring out the savoury best in the Romanian.

What slaves we are to our prejudices when it comes to matters of appetite.

Lie 4: *With fish you must drink white wine*

Complete tosh, this one. And I learned the lesson the hard way when I was once sitting in a French restaurant waiting for my cassoulet and sipping (or should I say, rather, chewing?) wine poured from my bottle of Cahors, and the very old man sitting opposite the unsettlingly young and disturbingly pretty woman at his table – which was barely a foot away from my own – ordered his turbot and his companion's to be cooked rare so that 'the bones show up pink' and to go with this he told the *sommelier* to bring a bottle of 1949 Chateau Pape Clement. This was in 1972.

I was thunderstruck. A red Graves, and an old one at that, with a half-cooked *Rhombus maximus*? Unbelievable. But do you know something? That old man and his young guest had the most marvellous time. They loved the food; they adored the wine; they laughed fit to burst at each other's *bons mots*. And here was me, a young Turk, with his regulation cassoulet and dutiful Cahors, and I thought to myself, I am being taught a great lesson in how to live here and it would be a crime not to remember it. And indeed I have remembered it.

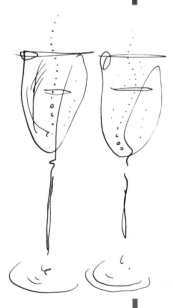

Now, I cannot say that I relish the idea of old Bordeaux with grilled flatfish, but if it turns you on, go for it. There are no rules. There are only tastes and, as memorably as old men in restaurants, young men in South Africa have often offered me their Pinotage with grilled local seafood delicacies and the combination works perfectly. Indeed, as a rule you can drink any young, fresh, fruity wine like Pinotage from the Cape or Syrah from the Languedoc or Kekfrancos from Hungary or Blauer Zweigelt from Austria or Valpolicella Classico from Italy or Chinon or Bourgueil from the Loire or Pinot Noir from Alsace with fish. Serve the wine lightly chilled and the effects will be even better.

Lie 5: *The excise duty on wine is desirable to deter excessive drinking and economically essential to maintain the liquidity of the Exchequer*

I find it difficult to maintain an even temper when statements like the above are aired. To begin with, wine drinkers are rarely drunkards. It is much more common to find beer and spirits drinkers who fall, literally, into the category of the inebriate. Nevertheless, wine is an alcohol and thus the duty levied on it is in part so levied because wine-drinking is seen as a frivolous luxury, and inessential to decent living, and therefore justifiably taxable. This is an old-fashioned and even dangerously unhealthy viewpoint. It is now proven that moderate red wine drinking confers positive health benefits (more of this on page 161). Thus, in taxing red wine excessively, many people are denied the opportunity to drink as much red wine as they might otherwise do to the extent of positively helping boost their health prospects. Supermarkets have done much, and are continuing to do much, to make wine widely available and easy to buy but still the Exchequer takes over £1 in duty and a big chunk in VAT. We can perhaps live with the VAT, but how many people are not living today, or not living as fully as they might, because that obscenely high rate of excise duty puts regular moderate wine drinking beyond their means?

A swingeing level of duty on wine is part of exactly the same dubious and restrictive moral universe as prohibition. (And even

> **❛ A swingeing level of duty on wine is part of exactly the same dubious and restrictive moral universe as prohibition. ❜**

when such a thing as total prohibition on alcohol was enforced in America, red wine was still legally purchasable at pharmacies for use by angina sufferers. The effects of wine as a medicine have been known for 5000 years. Only in the past fifty, and increasingly in the past ten, has there been precise scientific evidence as testament to its efficacy.)

If a British government recognized these facts and reduced duty, would there be a significant shortfall in revenue? I believe not. I base this belief on my expectation that if duty was drastically reduced, more people would drink regularly and buy more bottles; but if, added to this, VAT was adjusted, as sales taxes ought to be, so that the percentage increased as the wine rose in price – so that wines under £3 attracted a bottom rate of sales tax of 10 per cent rising to 15 per cent on wines at £5 through to a full 100 per cent on wines which cost £20 and more – the shortfall on income could be minimal.

Wine, to those who do not have a physical intolerance of its alcohol or other rational objection to it, is an essential adjunct to a civilized and healthy lifestyle. By taxing it as we do, we British are denying it its proper place in our society. Wine is a liquid food largely, though not exclusively, to be enjoyed with more solid food. The argument for taxing it to the extent that we do is no more valid and reasonable than if cut bread were to attract an excise tax of 5p a slice.

Lie 6: *Cheap own-label bottles of supermarket wine are perfunctory and undistinguished and never splendid*

This remains, surprisingly, a widespread delusion. I still hear the occasional cry, when I recommend a certain wine: 'Oh, I want something special, I don't want an own-label wine.' This misguided viewpoint goes back to the days when supermarkets did not employ the skilled professional wine buyers that they do now and merely bought any old filth and thus, in that faraway age when men thought a trolley was something which brought the drinks around, own-label wines were basic, crude, and nowhere near as well made as they are today. Supermarkets were also non-interventionist in those days. They didn't work hand-in-hand with wine-makers as they do now to create wines specific to their needs and tailored to the requirements of their customers. Wines today are of greater technical stability and cleanliness than ever before. And this applies to the cheapest bottle of own-label plonk.

But by no means all these wines are outstanding as well. Some are merely very drinkable, more are just good, basic, plonking, but there are also certain own-labels, widely available, which are just plain terrific. I refer to the own-label red and white Chilean wines on sale, at around £3.20 (or less) at Tesco, Asda and Sainsbury.

' Wine is an essential adjunct to a civilized and healthy lifestyle. '

The level of elegance and sheer silky fruitiness of these wines is really quite remarkable for the money. I truly feel at times, when confronting some stubborn cuss on the subject, that if I were to take any of these wines and pour them into an empty but much more fancily labelled wine, Chateau This or Domaine That, then he would pay twice the price and think himself very well suited and fruited into the bargain.

These Chilean own-label wines are usually blends of two grape varieties and also, sometimes, of two vintages. But the level of consistency I have observed in these wines over the past three years has impressed upon me that their blending, with supermarket buyers working so closely with the wine-makers on the ground, is the key to this consistency. Often, when the new vintage from wines declaring themselves in this way is not as good as it was, the blended own-label wines from the supermarkets have always been up to snuff.

The whites are always solid, everyday drinking and also fine with all manner of fish and chicken dishes as well as first-course vegetable salads. The reds, whilst perhaps not so robust that they can flirt with highly flavoured food, certainly exhibit the depth of fruit to accompany dinner-party roasts and grills happily. When I have a large gathering around the family dinner table I invariably pour half-a-dozen of such reds into two large jugs for people to help themselves, and almost without fail I will hear that comforting whisper in my ear, 'Well, Malcolm old fruit, you've certainly excelled yourself with this wine and I thought you only served up plonk.'

'Yes', I say, 'I thought I'd make an exception since you were invited and so I opened something really special.'

And I'm not telling one word of a lie.

Lie 7: *The way to make money from wine is to buy it ahead of bottling and cellar it, when it becomes available, for the next ten years or more*

The laying down of wine arouses as strong emotions as the laying down of the law. So let me ask you this: do you know how to make a small fortune from wine? Answer: start out with a large fortune.

This is a cute joke but it is also accurate. And nowhere is its accuracy more telling than when it comes to those dunderheads who acquire wine *en primeur*, as it is known in France, and to those merchants in this country which deal in it, which involves committing yourself to buying wine of a particular new vintage before it goes widely on sale in the shops. The hope is that this wine, which you may have neither seen nor tasted, will be greatly enhanced in value at some point in the future.

This is a gamble beside which the National Lottery is a speculative investment. The only way to buy wine is to taste it and decide for yourself that it is well priced and will age superbly in a measurable amount of time. Not all of us can make such judgments. You may rely on someone you trust, but the last person to listen to on the subject is the grower or wine-maker.

Overall, investing in wine for future accrual of value is a mug's game. The value is unlikely to materialize (except in exceptional instances involving ludicrously expensive collector's bottles which will only profit your descendants half a century from now when they auction the posthumous proceeds of your cellar) because the wine may not age as expected and the viability of such markets to maintain a consistent upward trend is not guaranteed (as many of those whose fingers were burned in the recent recession will testify). Wildly inflated claims for the future value of a particular wine will always be made but it is wise to ignore them. By all means lay down wine, in the right cool, dark conditions, to enjoy yourself in the future, but do this purely for your own personal pleasure not public profit. The practice is, in any case, largely irrelevant nowadays. Most of the wines we drink today are drinkable young and those that aren't liquidize into a comfortable middle age within five to seven years. There are, to be sure, wines which will always need two decades to hit their peaks – not just dessert wines and Cabernet-dominated blends from Bordeaux, Syrahs from the Rhône and Rieslings from Germany, but also red wines from Australia and California as well as Spain, Portugal and Italy. But in order to keep such genuinely fine wines you must be totally sure that the storage conditions are perfect, and few of us enjoy such privilege.

All this will fall on the wine collector's deaf-to-reason ears, of course. Men all over the world are cellaring wine in the same spirit of acquisitiveness as they garage vintage Bentleys and hang Picassos. Such men may never drink, rarely drive, or ever give their Pablos a second glance, yet

> ❛ **The only way to buy wine is to taste it and decide for yourself that it is well priced and will age superbly in a measurable amount of time…. Overall, investing in wine for future accrual of value is a mug's game.** ❜

they have created one of the silliest snobberies connected with wine. The idea that the only wines worth cellaring are exceedingly expensive, rarified bottles which must be carefully laid on their sides and shut away in cool, dark places to mature slowly into masterpieces is a plot to protect an investment. It has nothing to do with the fulfilling of a healthy appetite. It is crude showing off.

There is about this practice by wine collectors something of the Chinese custom, fashionable in years gone by, whereby those who were of the highest status in society allowed their fingernails to grow to such impossible lengths (some 70 inches was the longest recorded, though how this could be measured with the nails curling up and in on themselves is beyond my ken to figure out) that it was utterly impossible for the fingers attached to such monstrosities to carry out for themselves any manual work or even pursue simple household tasks, let alone, now that we have raised such an unpleasant though fascinating subject, ordinary personal tasks of hygiene. Such nails were advertisements. They instantly and evocatively broadcast to all who noticed them that here was a personage of rank and power. And so it is with the concept of the wine cellar and the wines collected to fill it.

We are dealing here with objects of status, which I despise. Such wines are not objects of pure quality, as assessed by that difficult and fluttering standard alone; they are merely monstrous fingernails created to flaunt a hierarchy – and an extremely dubious hierarchy at that.

It is undoubtedly true, nevertheless, that many wines do benefit from aging, and the ultimate pleasure they afford the drinker is greatly enhanced by allowing the amalgam of fruit and acid and, in the case of red wines, tannin also, to more progressively cohere, soften and become smoother as time passes. There is, though, a good deal of difference to my way of thinking between wines which are grown and fermented specifically to allow their ultimate purchasers to indulge in the sport of cellaring and wines which by their very nature will become more interesting beverages over a period of time.

I believe that with wines like expensive white burgundies, say, the barrel-fermentation and wood-aging processes force them to become creations which only time in bottle will make drinkable – if at all. Such processes mask the insufficiency of the fruit, the high yield of the vineyard, and even, in some cases, conceal the less than immaculate method of wine-making. With many reds, particularly those from Bordeaux which have a high tannin content and are well wooded, their astringency and austerity in youth make them harsh companions (even drunk with rich foods).

I except from this censure several of the Merlot-dominant wines from St Emilion and Pomerol, Premieres Cotes de Bordeaux, Graves, and Fronsac et al., but the fact that so many other wines, mainly of the Médoc, are intended for a market consisting largely of individuals who regard them as status symbols to be cooed over in cellars and to be flashed as conversational jewels means that judgment is always postponed. These wines are dreams (by which, as Chateaubriand pointed out, men are always successfully governed) and rarely considered as realities. I am not blind to their virtues, when these are apparent, but too few times are they so apparent. Only twice in my wine-drinking life have I encountered bottles which might have justified such reputations (but never their vast outlay) and these were a 1947 Chateau Margaux drunk in 1966, which was aromatically wondrous, and a Chateau Lafite 1934 drunk in 1984 which, though slightly austere (still!) from the tannin overlapping the fruit, did go brilliantly, it must be admitted, with a whole Bresse chicken roasted with forty cloves of garlic. The only unreservedly brilliant bottle of great wine I have ever drunk (also with chicken) was the red burgundy referred to in the introduction to this book.

The sort of wines I would recommend the drinker to lay down are those which offer the *possibility* of a highly delicious outcome along with the certainty of a highly deflated outlay. What guarantee have you that this possibility will become a reality? No guarantee whatsoever if you do not possess a cool, dark place, untouched by great fluctuations in temperature, where the wine can lie on its side so that the liquid touches

the cork across the full extent of its bottom. This last point is essential to prevent the cork drying out and air entering. If it does to any extent the wine will cheerfully, over time, turn itself into acetic acid. The cork itself is hardly a guaranteed 100 per cent foolproof method of sealing a bottle of wine either, so you may be disappointed on that score. I once bought a case of Rhône red, a curiously wonderful wine called Brezeme, from an impeccable source, the splendid firm run by Robin Yapp in Mere, Wiltshire. Robin specializes in wines from this area and twenty-six years ago personally introduced me to its rarer wines, yet nine of the twelve bottles were faulty because the corks suffered from tainting.

Nevertheless, if you are determined to lay aside a few bottles to see in the Millennium in four years' time and beyond, I can suggest where to find the most suitable candidates. On the white side, the 1994 Gewurztraminers from Alsace (especially the £4.99 bargains available at the larger stores) and the Tokay Pinot-Gris of 1993 and 1994 will develop an enhanced spiciness; the last three vintages of Chenin Blancs and Vedelhos and the various blends of these grapes – plus Chardonnay – from Western Australia will deepen and develop bouquet; Rieslings from New Zealand of the '92, '93 and '94 vintages (but not necessarily the '95s which seem more immediate drinkers to me at time of writing) will flaunt more vivacious fruit; from England – yes, England! –I would keep just one wine and that would be this coming November's Early Release from Three Choirs in Gloucestershire which, unless there is a disaster in this vineyard, should be a decent wine and will age, like others I have pulled from my coalhole, into a much more graceful and fascinating beast after five years in bottle; and early '90s vintages of Cava, Cremant d'Alsace, Cremant de Bourgogne and any of the cheaper supermarket non-vintage champagnes and South African sparkling wines under a tenner will be smoother specimens by AD 2000.

Where the reds are concerned, I would look to areas like Corbières, the southern Rhône (and particularly Gigondas, Vacqueyras, and Lirac), the Bordeaux satellites such as Fronsac and Blaye and the Hautes Cotes, Cabernet Sauvignons from northern and central

Italy, the northern Spanish regions of Penedes, Costers del Segre, Valdepenas, Conca de Barbera, Priorato and Valdepenas, Cabernet and Merlot blends from Argentina, certain Periquita and Cabernet blends from the Ribatejo and Alentejo regions of Portugal, and as far as Australia is concerned I would go for Shiraz, Merlots, and Cabernet blends from Clare, Maclaren Vale, Victoria and Margaret River (though it must be said that the many contenders here cost well over £5). In South Africa, I would consider the Pinotage and Merlot and Cabernet blends (Kanonkop is the name which springs most readily to mind).

The characteristics to look for in wines which will age are, broadly, acidity in white and tannin in red. However, these are appallingly simplistic guidelines; the taster judging wine which might age winningly must discern the presence of that ineffable feature which I can only call *character*. And there must be balance (a wine out of balance in youth will not correct itself with age). There must also be fruit, and the potential of more complete fruit developing; and this fruit when it does emerge must not be arthritic and over the hill. None of these judgements can be made by the inexperienced drinker or those not used to looking for the signs. Even professional wine buyers of long standing may not have the necessary sensory qualifications to enable them properly to assess a wine which will successfully develop over years.

As for certifying 100 per cent the success of the outcome of keeping wine, forget it, Charlie. All I am prepared to state is that it's not as lost a cause as one of Jack Duckworth's three-legged nags (see *Coronation Street* – on the other channel) but it is a more imaginative use of your money than crazy dreams of bagging the National Lottery.

Lie 8: *The words Appellation Contrôlée on a bottle of wine confer an absolute guarantee of authenticity and first-class drinking*

A better guarantee of the drinkability of any wine than the

legendary Appellation Contrôlée on its label are the words 'Specially selected by Sainsbury's buyers to offer exceptional quality and value'. Whilst the first pair of words mean nothing more than that the wine purports to emanate from a particular region as designated by a centrally run wine bureau in France, the second, leaving aside its amusing implication that only those Sainsbury's wines so designated possess quality and value and the rest of the range lacks either virtue, actually means what it says. It is – and I'm sorry, Mr Sainsbury, but I can't entirely rid myself of the temptation to enjoy a further little chuckle at your firm's foibles about its labelling procedure – a genuine attempt, however clumsy and tritely worded, to state that the wine is above average and carefully chosen.

This is precisely what many drinkers of French wines imagine those legendary French words above convey. But nothing could be further from the truth. Appellation Contrôlée simply means a controlled name. That is, the wine so named comes from the region given (if, say, it is a large expanse of vineyard like Languedoc-Roussillon) or, if a specific vineyard site is mentioned, then the wine comes from that place and no other. It is, of course, entirely possible that some of the wine in such bottles does not all come from the region or vineyard so named (please refer to page 24 for how this can come about) because someone involved in the production is a mountebank. But I am not concerned here with the likelihood of fraud or plain trickery but with the much more subtle machinations of perception versus reality.

When I first discovered wine, in my gullible year 1964, I was told by the first wine merchant from whom I bought and who managed, thankfully, to give me a lifelong abhorrence of his breed (apart from certain exceptions who do not fit the norm), that what AC meant was not only absolute integrity of origin but that a sample of the wine had been tasted by regional experts and pronounced to be a perfect example of both area and grape. Now in those days, the so-called great names of wine were not prohibitively expensive as they are today and I did enjoy some wonderful wines while swallowing a complete fabrication. Yet many drinkers I talk to today believe as I once did; they genuinely accept the idea that AC means quality as attested by experts.

Incredibly, you are better off believing hype than putting your faith in a set of wine laws which do not designate quality and do not represent as a matter of routine value for money.

Lie 9: *The letters MW after an individual's name indicate incomparable wine knowledge and expertise*

'*Nothing worth knowing can ever be taught.*' Oscar Wilde

I would estimate that at least 10 per cent of the time I am asked if I have a professional qualification for the work that I do. Are you a Master of Wine? is the question. No, I reply, why? Oh, no reason really – I just assumed that being an expert you … er. And there the question is dropped.

Not a soul ever asks if I am professionally qualified to write. It simply wouldn't occur to anyone. You can either write or you can't and, hopefully but not certainly, I would like to think that no one asks me the question, because the answer lies in my writing itself. Why then should it be necessary for some people to believe that wine knowledge is so special that it requires professional study and enletterment in order to write about it? It is easy to see why those in the wine trade should wish for some kind of qualification to ease them up the greasy pole of their career, and, in fact, that is the origin of the Institute of Masters of Wine. The exams involve five written papers and three wine-tastings where candidates sniff, swill and spit and attempt to guess the wines' provenance, and it is further expected that students will know all about the commercial realities of wine retailing, from the bottling of wine to the trucking of it. And this is as it should be since, one or two wine writers excepted, MW is a qualification which only those in the wine trade would seek to acquire (though I do believe there is an American film lawyer who has gone to the trouble, for some extraordinary reason, of acquiring it).

At bottom, the idea that a MW is a fount of all wine wisdom is bound up with the British and ex-colonial reverence for the so-called wine expert, where wine is seen as an arcane area only a chosen few have the ability to visit. In this rarified atmosphere, wine knowledge is as respected as the mystical ability to be fluent in a dozen tongues or the mental skill to master the maths for quantum mechanics in your head. Yet a person so magnificently multilingual or so prodigious at sums would not necessarily be able to say anything remotely worth hearing in any of his or her dozen languages, nor would he or she be able to use those maths to tell you the secret of the universe. In other words, those things that you'd *really* like to hear might well be beyond them. So it is with a Master of Wine.

In practice, the letters MW are no more a guarantee that their possessor knows a decent wine when it is under his or her nose than the letters ACCA are a guarantee that their holder will be able to spot a financial fraud when it is an open book. Now, understand me clearly here. I do not wish to denigrate the area of genuine specific scholarship which a successful MW candidate may be required to knuckle down to, but the deskbound qualification is simply irrelevant when compared with what I believe should be the true twin worths of the retail MW: first, to spot corked, dud or downright crappy wines and, second, to buy brilliant ones.

I have in the past encountered wines which are clearly corked at wine-tastings organized, in part, by Masters of Wine employed by retailers and merchants. How is it that these fellows did not spot the duds? I am unable to say. I often encounter wines in these circumstances which I think not just poor value for money but really poor specimens of wine altogether. This actually flies in the face of the MW charter which commits holders as part of a code to retail only wines of quality. I respect anyone with the stamina to pass a set of exams which represents genuine expertise and mastery of a subject, but do not ask me to consider that MW after my name would make me any better at *my* job.

Indeed, I have a hunch that it would make me a darn sight worse.

Lie 10: *You are better off paying £4.99 for a bottle of wine than £2.99*

In an attempt to snap back at the supermarkets and high street wine chains (but more especially the former) which have so voraciously chewed up the rule-book according to which only pretentious wine merchants with bright bow-ties standing in front of stacks of high-priced bottles are fit to retail wine, these same merchants, along with the wine hacks and critics who dine off the crumbs of their benevolence, have attempted over the past three years to mount a campaign to vilify inexpensive wines because they cannot compete with them. Hypocritically, the basis for their argument against cheap bottles is based on the high level of excise duty on wine which they claim to find so unfair and damaging.

Every bottle of wine, whatever its final retail price, whether that be £2.99 or £15.99, is subject to over £1 in duty (this is a fixed rate but the amount of the final sales tax which is added, via VAT, is variable, and so this also increases the financial burden on the final purchaser). However, clearly in a cheaper bottle of wine a greater proportion of the final purchase price goes in duty than with a more expensive bottle. Is it reasonable, the merchants' argument now runs, to give so high a proportion of the purchase price of a cheap wine to the parasites at the Exchequer? If you paid only a quid or two quid more you would not only be handing those parasites considerably *less* a proportion of the final purchase price but proportionately more could be returned to the original producer to be invested in the product.

This is an utterly fallacious line of argument. It is designed to make customers feel better about spending more on a bottle of wine (and thus to feel more benignly disposed towards merchants' higher prices). It has no substance because it is no guarantee of a better wine on the basis of the greater return available to the producer. This is because the greater proportion of the final purchase price *of an individual bottle* which goes back to the wine's actual producer is irrelevant in ensuring that the basic wine will be better because more money has been invested in it. Of course, the proportion of each *single* bottle sold of the cheaper wine which is returned as income to the original producer is less than with a more expensive bottle, but the producer is not concerned with individual bottles. It is the total sold which is the meaningful statistic. A producer will make *more* money with the cheaper wine because there will be many more bottles sold: 5000 cases of a £4.99 wine sold in a year might bring in the producer around £60,000, assuming that £1 on each bottle goes back to him; 100,000 cases of a £2.99 wine sold in a year could bring in the producer £240,000 on the basis that a mere 20p on each bottle is the producer's cut.

This is why so many supermarket bottles of £2.99 wine are so tremendously good. Everyone involved in the deal is making a healthy return because the turnover is respectable. The great majority of these bottles are denied to wine merchants because they are the subject of exclusive negotiated deals involving individual supermarkets and high street wine chains solely. I do not despise those general wine merchants who deal in small parcels of high-priced wines of equally high quality and true complexity, nor do I speak ill of those specialists who handle small producers' wines from particular regions. The impressive individuality of certain of these wines is deserving of the £10 or £15 price tags which they must, of economic necessity, flaunt.

But the delicious drinking bottle, likely as not own–label, at £2.99 or less is alive and well, and kicking many fat, lazy wine merchants in an area not unadjacent to their pockets where they feel it most keenly. There are also some truly fine bottles on sale, which stand comparison with wines costing many times more, between £3 and £4 – also mostly at the large retailers which can sell the quantities necessary to make a respectable return. Do not listen, then, to squeals from the wine establishment and their lubricious lackeys about the virtues of the higher-priced bottle. They are blathering through their bruised backsides.

Lie 11: *Australia will never turn out great Sauvignon Blanc*

Stroll on. One wine, from an area and from a producer more famous for chardonnay, refutes this old-fashioned idea with one sip. The wine is **Rosemount Reserve Sauvignon Blanc 1995** from the Hunter Valley. It costs

£6.50 at Tesco, Unwins and Wine Cellar and it is a mouth-wateringly scrumptious, refreshing, complex, concentrated and daz-zlingly elegant wine. I rather suspect that many Sauvignon producers, from the Loire as well as New Zealand, have been quite pleased that Australia, and specifically an area of such burgeoning reputation as the Hunter Valley, was deemed to be unsuitable territory for Sauvignon Blanc. But Rosemount, which also produces world-class Chardonnays, demonstrates that with this '95 vintage the Hunter can turn out world-class Sauvignon as well. I appreciate, alas, that the '95 may no longer be on sale at this point in time (and if it is, then it is certainly a more mature and less impactfully refreshing and frisky an animal than it was when I first tasted it). The '96 should now be available, but since the grapes for it were only being picked as this book was on its way to the printer, you will, I am sure, forgive me for not providing an assessment of this latest vintage in these pages.

Lie 12: Wine was much better in the old days

There are lots of things which were better in the old days but wine is not one of them. Never before in the whole history of wine have we in this country had access to such technically accomplished, cheap, fruity, complex, and altogether more healthy wines. The cleanliness of modern wine-making techniques, the improvement in vineyard management concepts, the widespread use of ideas which reduce reliance on excessive use of chemicals (from pesticides in the vineyard to sulphur in the finished wine) mean that the ordinary bottle of everyday drinking wine on the supermarket shelf is more stable than it was twenty- five years ago. Cheap wine in the old days was largely, though not exclusively, pretty naff stuff. Nowadays we've never had it so good.

Lie 13: Wine drinking is bad for you and it is healthier to stick to water

'*Always remember that I have taken more out of alcohol than alcohol has taken out of me.*' Winston Churchill

Wine was originally conceived and utilized as a medicine. Early humans, having observed the warming effects of the liquid on the body and the change which came over its imbibers, entirely correctly inferred from this that it had, unless the dosage was so large as to make the drinker ill

> ❛ There are lots of things which were better in the old days but wine is not one of them… Cheap wine in the old days was largely, though not exclusively, pretty naff stuff. Nowadays we've never had it so good. ❜

or insensible, a beneficial effect. Today, we have scientific evidence suggesting very strongly that moderate regular drinking of wine, particularly red, has a positive effect on health. Wine is a food. True, it is also a alcohol and alcohol, like all drugs, can produce the allergy of addiction in those who should go nowhere near it. But if we were to treat with suspicion and shun everything in life which can be abused, none of us would pick up a telephone for fear of running the risk that an obscene caller was on the other end.

Red wine contains substances (along with phenolic constituents like tannin) which can help reduce blood-clotting and the narrowing of the arteries. It can reduce cholesterol, thereby helping to lessen the risk of certain heart conditions occurring. Wine of any colour is also an aid to digestion. Indeed, one wine has been said to have been an aid to procreation.

This wine is called **Frank's Big Red** (now joined by a white). It costs £3.99 at Victoria Wine. It is a massively fruity concoction from Minervois in southern France made by an American chemist of Polish extraction who was shipwrecked and met and married a local *vigneron*'s daughter. When I first tasted this wine, and read about its making, I scribbled various things about it in my wine notebook which I intended to turn into an article. I didn't write it in the end. But the substance of my notes reads as follows:

When I was in California I was told by several wine-growers that the morning after the American publication of the French find-ings on the benign relationship between red wine and heart disease they were besieged by crowds desperate to buy this suddenly magical elixir. We European swiggers hardly need to be told that wine is a healthy pastime if not taken to embarrassing extremes but Americans require, it would appear, the incentive of documented proof of instant immortality in order to drop their awful beer-swilling habits for the alchemical effects of the grape. In the light of such behaviour, Frank's Big Red will, should any bottle find its way Stateside, cause nation-

wide rioting — a reaction which will cause no surprise to the wine's manufacturer, Frank Chludinski, since, being an American himself, he is presumably fully conversant with his countrymen's and women's gullibilities. The wine is exclusive to Victoria Wine, which asks a not unreasonable £3.99 for it, and a thoroughly enjoyable, rich, earthy and biggish red it is, with a delicious rounded smoothness and softness yet robustness which typifies the best wines from this region. It also throws in for good measure a feral herby quality. However, it is the miracle told on the back label which would cause transatlantic stampedes, for it quotes a letter received by Mr Chludinski from a very grateful friend and customer who reveals that after drinking quantities of Big Frank's Red he successfully impregnated his wife after 'many years of trying'. What this letter does not say, but which the vendor tells me is true, is that this epistolic stud is a man of seventy and his wife twenty. I shall leave aside the interesting question of quite how many years this couple had been trying for parenthood and rate Big Frank's Red as a simple, entertaining beverage of forceful style and rugged fruitiness.

Wine drinking, then, sensibly indulged in, is a healthy, civilized, even fruitful pursuit. There really is no more to be said. (Oh, yes there is. Cheers!)

Six Questions I'm Always Asked

The postman has cause to rue my address. He has to lug a lot of letters to it — mostly from readers. Readers represent a fecund vine. The yield is enormous. Readers throw loads of questions at me; and these, along with the posers put to me face to face when I do my usual autumnal nationwide bookshop tour, provide much fruitful food for thought. The six most often asked questions are these:

1. Is Gluck your real name?

2. What is tannin?

3. Do you really taste all those wines?

4. Do you need an assistant?

5. Don't you ever get tiddly?

6. What is your favourite wine?

1. *Is Gluck your real name?*

All the physical defending I was scholastically involved in because of my surname (courtesy of a Viennese grandfather) often made me wish for the anonymity of a Smith or a Jones. These attacks on my good name took no note of its meaning (which I was assured, bizarrely and most inappropriately in my view, meant happiness) or the possibility that one day I would become a wine writer and some bright spark at the BBC would put two and two together (and get three Glucks).

I rather regret the amount of blood spilled in my defence of Happiness but, now at least, I wouldn't change my moniker for all the Chardonnay in the Côte d'Or (though if you make that all the Chardonnay in the Upper Hunter I might consider it).

2. What is tannin?

I like any amount of tannin in red wine. I like it in very small doses in tea. I like it in wine because it gives a texture to the fruit which permits food to be caught on it, and it provides a solid framework for that fruit and deepens it. Often tannin is a coarse element in the texture of the wine (in a young Cabernet Sauvignon from Bordeaux, say) but it may be less virulent in a warm New World area (where the skins of the grapes have not naturally grown thick to protect themselves from cold Atlantic winds), and the substance itself can be fined out with egg whites to a greater or lesser extent, since it is soluble and capable of extraction. Over time in bottle, tannin will turn to sediment and the wine soften as a result.

Tannin is, then, one of several manoeuvrable chemical aspects of the liquid under the wine-maker's control. Tannin also, according to some medical opinion, contributes to wine as a health drink (since it increases its effectiveness as an antioxidant, anti-blood-clotting agent and can help in building resistance to heart complaints). And tannin also provides the potential, along with acidity, for a wine to age, often for a spectacularly long time with stunning results.

Tannin is one of several chemical constituents produced in the wine-making process, so-called phenolic compounds, and it is more prevalent in red wine than white because much of it is derived from the skins (also pips and stalks) of the grapes and it is from the skins that wine gets its colour, the grape pulp itself being pale. Tannin also emanates from the new wood in which some wines are aged (thus a barrel-fermented or oak-aged Chardonnay will contain tannin but this will never be so noticeable as with a red wine because of the greater gentility of wood tannin over fruit-derived tannin and also because of the higher acidic sensation of a white wine over a red).

Tannin is so called because it turns skin into leather – it tans it. It is for this reason that the inside of your mouth will feel dry and pucker up with a sensation of shrinkage. The tannin is doing its job. It is literally tanning your mouth (and leaving a most distinctive black scum on your teeth). Most drinkers new to wine dislike tannin and even find it intimidating in richly fruity grape varieties like Syrah or the wonderful, soupily rich French southern reds made from the Tannat grape, where tannin levels give the romanticist the notion that he will live for ever and his heart never stop. Tannin can have this effect on the mind? Tannin can have this effect on the mind.

3. Do you really taste all those wines?

This question is asked in reference to my wine guides where several thousand wines are listed and drunk afresh every year. I taste many more wines than are listed in either book. I taste my way through many hundreds of bottles a month. I drink and enjoy several glasses of wine every day. I taste lots of the wines I write about with food. My average consumption, curiously, is probably not more than a bottle a day. During intensive tastings I am, of course, assessing wines without swallowing much more than a fraction of a teaspoon.

4. Do you need an assistant to help you drink all those wines?

Thank you for the offer, but no. It is true that other wine-guide writers employ others to help them compile their works and some of them actually taste in teams. I employ a part-time secretary to help with my correspondence and to run my computer back-up system (with all those thousands of wines on dozens of disks an Apple a day is essential). I also employ a part-time researcher.

But no one can help me taste wine. Be suspicious of all judgements about wine made by teams or pairs of tasters. Individual judgment is more important because it is purer and freer of taint. It is judgement free of others' interference and clumsy consensus.

This is not to say that an individual is less likely to make an error. Only that the individual taster is more likely to be him or herself. And I believe that is what readers want: the views and judgements of an individual expressing personal preferences and dislikes. It is only to an individual, after all, that the individual reader/drinker can relate and develop a relationship based on trust through an understanding of what that individual wine writer personally likes and dislikes. I am far from infallible but I do know what I like.

What I like is unpretentious wine, fruity, purposeful, ungilded by excessive wood or the cosmetics of an over-zealous wine-maker, and, above all, I want that wine to be priced properly. That is my single unwavering focus.

> ❛ What I like is unpretentious wine, fruity, purposeful, ungilded by excessive wood or the cosmetics of an over-zealous wine-maker, and, above all, I want that wine to be priced properly.... If the wine writer serves any useful purpose it is that he or she is a single conduit through which all those thousands of bottles on shelf can be filtered and the best ones given a chance to be discovered by drinkers everywhere. ❜

If the wine writer serves any useful purpose it is that he or she is a single conduit through which all those thousands of bottles on shelf can be filtered and the best ones given a chance to be discovered by drinkers everywhere. For those who enjoy reading what I write about wine, I am simply that conduit.

5. Don't you ever get tiddly?

Yes. I enjoy wine so much that I find it impossible to resist, now and then, some stratospherically highly fruity red (a 14 per cent Zinfandel from California, perhaps) after I have already enjoyed a white wine and possibly a few glasses of sparkling wine, and since I also approve of Calvados (and often have a glass before turning in for the night) this may be why, after a while, I feel that I am in no state to jump on my bike or play two sets of tennis. Chess is the best pastime, I find, once this stage has been reached. Indeed, the frivolity of chess is the one thing I'm fit for at such times; it is the only game in the world which should only be played after one has consumed at least a bottle of wine (and if such a rule was introduced into grandmaster games it would enliven proceedings considerably). It also has the advantage of being a game you can enjoy while simultaneously researching the contents of a glass of wine.

6. What is your favourite wine?

The one in my glass at the time the question is put.

If, however, I was being taken out and guillotined in the morning (for my crime of speaking so little French with any fluency that even as simple an exhortation as 'Call this a £70 bottle of Romanee St-Vivant? It's so feeble it's barely fit to mull' I can only express in my native English), then I would drink **Ridge California Zinfandel Lytton Springs 1992.** This magnificent wine can sometimes be found at Oddbins and Majestic Wine Warehouses. It costs around £15. It represents great value for money.

10 Do SuperMarket Wine Buyers Know Their Onions?

'Tis with our judgements as our watches, none go just alike, yet each believes his own.' Alexander Pope, Essay on Criticism, 1711

Intimate knowledge of the edible bulb *Allium cepa* rather than deep understanding of Pinot Noir or, say, fluency in the language of Germany, is precisely what gets up the noses of various so-called (i.e., self-designated) wine experts who, pouring ill-informed scorn as liberally as they lap up ill-formed wine, express their disdain of those supermarket wine buyers who previously purchased vegetables (or electric light bulbs) before moving on to the wine department. I can feel indifferent to these prats' predilection for raddled vino, though I cannot deny my sense of astonishment, thinly disguised as amusement, as they pontificate about a patently ill-kempt burgundy, a vastly overpriced and monodimensional sweet bordeaux, or a champagne which is demonstrably thin on fruit and thick on price.

However, the denigra-  tion of the super- market wine buyer (as distinct from the high street wine chain wine buyer) I do feel a mea- sure of passion about.

These critically self-serving, pompous, hollow wine Johnnies and Janes feel nervous, and doubtless a touch redundant and unwanted, at the way supermarkets have placed a premium on buyers' negotiating skills rather than specific wine knowledge. Experts and professions are always closed shops, and thus for the inhabitants of these shops and their various lackeys, among whom I lump many wine critics, to be witness, for example, to the nation's most active wine merchant, J Sainsbury plc (now selling 100 million bottles of wine a year), cheerfully recruiting the new manager of its wine-buying department from the meat and delicatessen counter sticks in the throat. It is outrageous. It is a slur on established practice and a slight on professionalism.

The simple fact is, however, that supermarkets like Asda, Morrison, Safeway, Sainsbury, Somerfield, Tesco and all the others have established their hegemony as the prime merchants of wine in this country precisely *because* of this focus on buyers' buying skills above all else. It is true that Waitrose only employs wine buyers able to append MW after their name (see page 155), thus signifying that they have passed the Master of Wine exams and are members of the Institute of Masters of Wine. Other supermarkets also have MWs on their staff, and some of these buyers, particularly the old hands at Asda, Morrison and Somerfield, have experience of wine at other retail outlets. So the general criticism that buyers are recruited who have no specific wine knowledge is only true of certain individuals.

It is a fact that German wine buyers do exist who speak no German, and there are New World wine buyers who know more about pâtisserie than they do about phylloxera (a microscopic vine pest). This grates, but since the individuals who are the cause of the grating are in every instance supervised by higher managers of considerable expertise, it seems that a good deal of fuss is being made about what is a minor issue. Or is it in truth the symptom of a much larger concern? Is it elsewhere that we must look for the *real* source of the irritation?

The wine prats are irritated because their own irrelevance and insignificance are thrown in their faces. The wine revolution orchestrated by the supermarkets and enthusiastically carried on by the big wine chains has succeeded in reducing the importance of and diluting the energy of the old wine establishment which so many wine critics serve (if listlessness, torpor and marketing *ennui* can be said to generate any energy), and it is this which is at the heart of these critics' concerns. Every single innovation aimed at making wine more popular, more widely available and more of a simple everyday pleasure rather than a ritual which only the chosen can understand, has been opposed by the prats. They hate:

1. Flying wine-makers. (They should be shot down before they land. How dare an Australian pitch up in Italy or France or Portugal and turn the charmingly undrinkable local filth into clean, fruity, CHEAP wine.)

2. All wines under £3.49. (Poor old Justin Timefora-Largeport with his shelves full of twelve-quid reds and eight-quid whites can't compete. It is monstrously unfair.)

3. Wine writers who enthuse over wines under £3.49. (These people are vermin. They make expensive wine appear ridiculous and bring famous wine areas which have been happily ripping drinkers off for decades into disrepute.)

4. The whole idea of supermarkets being the nation's leading wine merchants. (Ugh! Imagine pushing a trolley made out of coathangers and choosing your own wine instead of having a failed estate agent ineptly masquerading as a wine merchant palming you off with clumsy clarets at a tenner a bottle.)

They also despise any wine not sealed with a cork and hate wine boxes (both these icons are covered elsewhere in this book, along with a good deal of the other prejudices the wine revolution is slowly stripping away from the British attitude to wine). As far as flying wine-makers are concerned, it will be quite obvious to even the casual reader of this book that many of the wines I recommend highly are made by these peripatetic and, at least as far as historical processes are concerned, only mildly revolutionary creatures. The flying wine-maker, employed by the supermarket or wine chain on assignment specifically to create a wine for them to retail, is merely a continuation of the centuries-old habit of British mercantile interference in wine-growing countries' local customs and practices. We British made champagne possible (firstly, because we liked the secondary ferment in bottle and inspired the French to persevere with it and, secondly, because the furnaces of Sir Kenelm Digby in Derbyshire were the first to generate the heat necessary to form glass of sufficient strength to withstand the atmosphere of pressure which develops, via carbon dioxide, inside a sparkling wine bottle). We created madeira, marsala, port (this last the only drink in the world made by ex-minor public-schoolboys). We influenced the styles of bordeaux, red and white burgundy, Rhine and Moselle Rieslings. We once ran some of the countries now producing so many of the most exciting wines in the New World (the USA, Canada, South Africa, New Zealand and Australia) and many of our trading strategies were directly responsible for fostering the early development of vineyards in these lands.

Not since the Romans has any nation been so influential in encouraging the spread of the vine and having such a huge input into the wine produced – and certainly to greater geographical and more lasting degree than the Romans. The flying wine-maker is merely carrying on the tradition. So why do the prats hate the idea? It can't be on grounds of injured national pride or historical pedigree. It can only be because the wines are sold so cheaply by supermarkets and high street wine shops. From this prejudice the other three stem.

Wines under £3.49 confer such bad value, if you judge

value by how big a proportion of the final price of the bottle is made up by excise duty. This argument, fallacious and transparently self-serving, attempts to persuade customers that they are better off spending a fiver or more on a bottle because that way they are contributing less in excise duty and more to the wine-grower. What is not mentioned in this equation is that more also goes to the merchant. It also ignores volume. The money made by a wine-maker who sells 50,000 cases of wine in a single negotiated lot to a super-market is greater than what he would make if he sold fifty lots of a thousand cases. This simple case of logic also holds water when it comes to the same wine-maker working out that he is better off, that is to say, makes more money, if he sells a million bottles a year to a supermarket (which sells them at £2.99) than considerably less than this to a greater number of retailers (who will price the wine at £4.99). I have covered this ground in more detail on page 157.

The sheer volume supermarkets deal in is the crucial factor here. That is to say, popularity of wines. This requires superb distribution and marketing skills. Old established wine merchants lack the verve to compete, not just the money. They would always prefer to deal in the unimaginative, the established, and the wine for which no marketing effort or flair is required. It is the wine merchants who do not duck hard work and who possess real talent, like Tanners and Adnams, say, who can still claim to offer competition to the supermarket and, more especially, the high street wine chain.

The supermarkets must offer genuine value for money or lose business. Never has the food and drink retailing scene in the UK been so furiously competitive. Small wonder the biggest players rate buying skills as more important than superficial (and often utterly irrelevant) knowledge.

Do supermarket wine buyers know their onions? The proof is in the pulling. The proof is in the brilliantly fruity, cheap wine which pulls in customers and keeps them coming back for more.

THE LONELY AND EXPENSIVE LIFE OF THE SINGLE GRAPE. ANSWER: MARRIAGE!

11

'I've sometimes thought of marrying – and then I've thought again.' Noel Coward, 1956

One of many interesting discoveries I made on my very first trip around the wine regions of Australia was how wine-makers came over all funny when I remarked, as I did now and then, how brilliantly the Semillon grape went with the Chardonnay. It became apparent that there was a certain embarrassment in some quarters about this union of varieties, and in bringing the matter up I was committing a *faux pas* – as if, indeed, I was going out of my way to point out a violent blot on an otherwise immaculate escutcheon which polite society would prefer to forget. The reason was that the average Australian wine drinker, stretched out on his sun lounger or poking the coals in his barbecue, had problems with the idea of putting Semillon with Chardonnay.

When I first tasted the examples of the blend, some years ago now, I was merely struck by how successful it was; the wines were rich, complex, balanced, and struck up a firmer relationship with many foods than either variety on its own might have done (which is in no way to denigrate the superb examples of

single-varietal Semillon and Chardonnay wines which Australia produces and which, I hope and expect, will never be blended). The marriage option had obvious advantages. It gave more strings to wine-makers' bows with regard to blending (more vineyards to choose from and more barrels to pick) and, hugely important this, it gave retailers in the UK access to more wine, more blending opportunities of their own, and thus prices would be driven downwards without in any way affecting quality.

But this is not how yer average Aussie saw it. 'Wot! You've gone and shoved Semillon in with your Chardonnay? Something wrong with the Chardonnay on its own was there? I want Chardonnay! By itself! I don't want it adulterated with another variety. It must be an inferior wine.'

It is also true to say that some British wine drinkers saw it like this, too. But in Australia there was considerable resistance to the idea because so many wine drinkers there had grown up with the idea that the single variety was best and that blending two, or several for that matter, was not adding anything but taking something away.

That anyone could take this line astonished me, but then the more I thought about it the more I could see how perfectly natural a response it was. It is a racial characteristic in English-speaking countries to pigeon-hole everything, and the human temperament in general is suspicious of change and doubtful about experimentation, particularly with regard to things we put in our mouths.

Personally, I was aghast when I first saw a bottle of **Bulgarian Vintage Blend Khan Krum Chardonnay and Sauvignon Blanc** (a little above £3 at supermarkets and high street wine shops). How could they put Sauvignon and Chardonnay together? Surely, it meant nothing more than that the Chardonnay was insufficiently acidic to stand alone and the Sauvignon improperly unfruity? What other motive could there be for the blend? I was acting no differently from the conservative Aussies. I did swallow my prejudices, however, when I tasted the wine, and recommend it heartily.

In a similar vein, I couldn't understand, initially, why the Cape wine-makers would blend Pinotage (which is already a blend of grapes in its own right since it is a crossing of Pinot Noir and Cinsault) with pure Cinsault. Wasn't this a blatant attempt to tamper with what was in my eyes, with regard to Pinotage, a wonderfully fruity variety which could stand alone? Yet here again on tasting the wine the added depth and tannic texture given the Pinotage by the addition of Cinsault increased complexity and power. You can find Pinotage/Cinsault blends at around £3.50 at several supermarkets and high street wine shops. I cannot say they are as richly inviting as certain 100 per cent Pinotage wines but they do offer one huge benefit. I'll come on to that in a moment.

The Frenchman and woman – married, young, sveltely dressed – who asked me to sign their copy of *Superplonk* (yes! It does sound unlikely but they were buying the book as a present for their English hosts) at a Coventry bookshop, and for whom I poured glasses of **Sainsbury's Romanian Merlot/Pinot Noir,** also reacted strongly when they saw Merlot and Pinot Noir together on the same label. '*Mon Dieu!* The grape of Burgundy and the grape of Bordeaux in the same wine! I have never seen this before. How extraordinary!'

But they slurped with enthusiasm and, initially surprised that Romania even had a wine industry let alone one which permitted nuptials between, in their view, the incorrigibly unmarriageable, very quickly made noises to the effect that at £2.85 this was a tremendous wine. They forgot any initial prejudice they

had when they tasted the wine because it was patently first-class – and an experience they intended to repeat as it would considerably enhance their first experience of being sent to Coventry.

I felt as this French couple did when I first saw **Fairview Estate Zinfandel/Cinsault 1995** from the Back family vineyards in South Africa. Zin and Cin?! No way, Jose. This seemed sacrilege indeed. But the wine is simply wonderful, full of spice and aroma, like the stuffing of a Christmas fowl, and at just under a fiver at Oddbins and £4.49 at Asda (which quickly ran out of it at that price), it was a festive bottle in its own right. It was also a bargain – at either price.

But why blend in the first place? The answer is provided by the last word of the previous paragraph.

Blending permits wine to be made cheaper. The single-varietal wine is often a luxury and, many times, not capable of standing on its own. I am quite sure that the Merlot/Pinot Noir blend was created when a supermarket buyer arrived at the winery in Romania and a negotiation along the following lines took place.

Buyer (taking out electronic calculator and flexing his fingers): Right. I'm interested in 40,000 cases of your Merlot and 30,000 cases of your Pinot Noir. I need to hit a price point in the UK of £2.99.

Winery Export Director (positioning even larger electronic calculator in front of him and impressively coaxing out of it, unobserved by the supermarket wine buyer, the first few bars of the overture to Smetana's rarely performed opera You'll Be Lucky, Squire*):* Wonderful! But I can only bottle you 20,000 cases of the Merlot and 18,000 cases of the Pinot Noir.

How does that sound? Do we have a deal?

> **❛ Blending permits wine to be made cheaper. ❜**

Buyer (fingers flash over the calculator — a grim, cold, hard look, like Transylvanian mountain frost, settles on his otherwise warm face): At those quantities we could only sell each wine at £3.39 to make our margins. Well, I'd best be off. How far is it to the winery at Dob Usinessatan Ycost?

Export Director: Will you be permitted to go there after the outbreak of plague in the area? Look. Taste this Merlot again. *(He gestures at the bottles and wine glasses within reach on the table.)* Try our Pinot Noir a second time. Are they not bargains for your customers at £3.39?

Buyer (in a theatrical gesture, to make a point, he pours his glass of Merlot into his glass of Pinot Noir): If only, Nicolae, we had one wine on the table and you had 38,000 cases of it, we could do business.

Wine-maker (who, although he sits just the other side of the table, has been quiet during the meeting — he speaks no English — now breaks his silence in outrage at the barbaric bringing-together of his Merlot and Pinot Noir in the same glass): Aaargh! Sob!

Buyer (picks up his glass of Merlot and Pinot Noir): Well! If I'm to survive the plague at Dob Usinessatan Ycost I need a stiff drink. Cheers!

End of story. It was quickly apparent to the buyer that the two wines were wonderful as one, and if 38,000 cases were available he could actually price it not just at £2.99 but at £2.85. The wines were in separate tanks and it was a simple business of putting the two together and pumping them into an empty tank. Of course, I exaggerate the ease by which the blend was arrived at; more likely, several blends, differing in proportions of one variety over another, were tried, and the wine-maker, less hostile once he saw how good a wine was coming out of the experiment, forgot his antipathies.

And who benefits in the end? We do. You and I. I think £2.85 is a splendid price to pay for an eminently drinkable, food-friendly, complex wine of character, style and richly inviting fruit, and it all helps to provide us with wines which we can truly afford as everyday drinking wines. True, the purist and the wine snob chafe at the ravishing of single-varietal individuality, but who cares? In the end, marriage works.

It also clearly works for the vineyards and wineries who supply UK retailers. They have a broader economic base for their operations, a more versatile portfolio of wines, more assured income, and greater flexibility in creating saleable wines when vintage conditions produce less than outstanding stand-alone qualities in a certain grape variety.

The American TV soap I saw an extract from recently, in which a pneumatically perfect blonde replied to a restaurant waiter's invitation to have a drink that she would have 'A Chardonnay, please,' sums up the problem with the single varietal route in a nutshell: single varietals become brands in their own right. I do not for one second wish a winery like Rosemount in the Hunter Valley to stop making its consistently wonderful Show Reserve 100 per cent Chardonnays (or its less brilliant but effective Chardonnay–Semillon blend) but for cheaper wines I am all in favour of ignoring grape varieties and concentrating instead on a name on the label which makes the variety, or the blend of varieties, irrelevant. Blending, the marriage of grape varieties, is one of the least exploited and least well-mastered arts available to the wine-maker.

> **Blending, the marriage of grape varieties, is one of the least exploited and least well-mastered arts available to the wine-maker.**

We will all be better off, and drink cheaper and better wine, when our fixation with the bachelor/spinster variety – single, unproductive and expensive – is relaxed.

WINE SNOBS AND THEIR BLADDER PROBLEMS

12

Not a pleasant subject, the bladder? Bear with me. You will end up with a source of wine supply which will enable you to enjoy a glass of fresh, fruity wine every day, for around 45p or less a glass, and yet you need never open another bottle or use a corkscrew, and certainly you will never again have to face the prospect of seeing wine you cannot drink, because you do not wish to finish what is left in the bottle, being thrown away or, better at least, used to beef up the gravy.

I refer, of course, to the much-maligned wine box. Quite why this should arouse the ire and the scorn of the snob defeats my understanding. To begin with, the historical lineage of the idea is impeccable. Was not wine in its first incarnation stored in asses' skins? Long before pottery containers were invented, and certainly eons before the mass-produced glass bottle arrived, early wine-makers used treated animals' stomachs, with a removable stopper, to transport wine for individual and group use. What, then, is so sacrilegious and barbarically modern about filling an airtight 3-litre plastic balloon with wine, adding an airtight tap, and sealing it inside a cardboard box?

True, when the idea first came along the wine was pretty dire and the technology was not perfect. But now the wine is first-rate and it really does stay fresh for four to five weeks once the tap has been turned. I can't say I always find it a simple business to extract the tap through its orifice in the cardboard when opening the box for the first time, and the storing of a white wine box in a small fridge which has other essentials in it is sometimes a cause of friction between an otherwise smoothly loving couple (I speak with feeling here). But it is a sound way to keep and to serve wine.

The wine box is also a barrier breaker. There is, I think, something infra dig about helping yourself at a party to the contents of a wine bottle but wine boxes left at strategic spots around a room, or in a garden, are more inviting to guests and save you the trouble of having to constantly prowl around with bottle in hand. Perhaps herein lies a clue to the critical misappreciation of the wine box. Just as they break barriers they also demystify wine and eliminate many of its rituals.

Wine boxes require no cellar. They do not ask to be laid on their side for years. They demand no corkscrew and no sniffing of any cork once opened. They defy conventional labelling. In other words, many of the time-honoured habits of the wine buff are redundant. The rites of our ancestors, so faithfully and mindlessly followed by wine snobs today, have no relevance when one is faced with the joys of the wine box.

Small wonder, now that we have given the matter a little thought, that certain stuffy wine drinkers feel uncomfortable with the idea of a wine in a box instead of a bottle. The wine box is the pea under the princess's bed; the cheerful agnostic – upright while everyone else unsmilingly bends the knee and inclines the head; the usurper. The wine box tosses out of the window at a stroke the ritualized traditions of centuries.

It is a pity our pubs do not keep a selection of wine boxes behind their bars. It would solve the problem of badly kept wine in such institutions. We all know how galling it is to ask for a glass of wine in the Flea and Fiddle and to be given an oxidized rancid puddle of fruit from a bottle which was first opened three weeks ago. Publicans do not need to go to any great trouble to acquire boxes. They need only nip down to the local supermarket. Retailer own-label boxes as well as some of the ones from Stowells offer good wine, and at pub prices the pubs could even afford to buy retail.

► **My favourite wine boxes are**
Bulgarian Cabernet Sauvignon (Sainsbury)
Cabernet Sauvignon Suhindol (Safeway)
Chardonnay Vin de Pays d'Oc (Sainsbury)
Corbieres (Sainsbury)
Le Vigneron French Red (Asda)
Le Vigneron French White (Asda)
Namaqua Dry White (Safeway)
Stowells Bulgarian Cabernet Sauvignon (Oddbins, Thresher, Victoria Wine, Waitrose)
Stowells South African Chenin Blanc (Morrison, Tesco, Thresher, Victoria Wine)
Stowells Chilean Merlot/Cabernet (Morrison)
Stowells Chilean Sauvignon Blanc (Morrison)
Stowells Mendoza Dry White (Waitrose)
Stowells New Zealand Sauvignon Blanc (Oddbins, Safeway, Somerfield, Tesco, Thresher)
Stowells South African Pinotage (Tesco, Thresher, Waitrose)
Stowells Australian Shiraz Cabernet (Asda, Safeway, Somerfield, Tesco, Thresher, Victoria Wine)
Stowells South African Sauvignon Blanc (Unwins, Waitrose)
Stowells Tempranillo La Mancha (Asda, Morrison, Safeway, Sainsbury, Tesco, Unwins, Waitrose)
Stowells Vin de Pays du Gard (Asda, Oddbins, Safeway, Somerfield, Thresher, Victoria Wine)
Stowells Vin de Pays du Tarn (Asda, Kwik Save, Oddbins, Safeway, Somerfield, Thresher, Victoria Wine)

These boxes are priced from around £10–£14.

13 THE ROMANTIC IDEA

Think you, if Laura had been Petrarch's wife,
He would have written sonnets all his life?'
Lord Byron, Don Juan.

Wine is a sensual experience or it is nothing. The least expensive and gentlest of fruity wines has *something* sensual about it, something which appeals to the senses in the most fundamental way, even if it is merely a component in a meal and is playing second fiddle to a plate of fresh eggs still hot from the hen which have been simply and deliciously scrambled. Of all red varieties, none is more sensual than Zinfandel and that is why I love it so much; rich, deep, tannic, leathery, potent, highly alcoholic at times but never off-puttingly so, and ineffably herby and warm and *of the soil.*

Zinfandel is California's grape. It is not California's alone (Chile and South Africa both turn out interesting specimens, and in Western Australia there are a whole six acres of it), but it is California's unique gift to express its fruit so vibrantly and vivaciously. I don't entirely deride the idea of grape varieties which are special to a particular region. If you have a grape variety you can call your very own, you've got the basis for incomparability. As long as you're making terrific wine consistently, vintage after vintage, you'll be loved. Even if one great vintage doesn't follow another, we drinkers will forgive you the odd lapse when the weather is disastrous. We can sentimentalize about old times and look forward to your next year's vintage which is bound to be better. The problems start when you get greedy or you take our affections for granted and get sloppy in the vineyard and slapdash in the winery and there is a run of poor vintages. An irrevocable slide sets in and we customers start to take notice of other regions making similar wine. And suddenly your grape variety isn't so exclusive any more. Then two things can happen: one, other regions take up your variety and grow it better, or, two, the variety becomes forgotten, unfashionable and, often unjustifiably, neglected by growers in other regions looking for something different to experiment with. The first example fits Sancerre, the second Muscadet.

The Loire and Fumé Blanc is a pairing now totally overshadowed by

> **'If you have a grape variety you can call your very own, you've got the basis for incomparability.'**

New Zealand and Sauvignon Blanc, which is what Fumé Blanc is. Sancerre and Pouilly Fumé, the Loire regions famous for white Sauvignon, have largely blown it. The grape variety is now made better by Chileans than by the growers in the Loire. Gewurztraminer and Alsace? Inseparable until the South Africans came along at the cheaper end of the market, although the '94 vintage for Alsace represents a solid and well-priced fightback at £4.99 a bottle. And certain great Gewurztraminers, particularly the sweet late-harvest examples, are uniquely exciting in their Alsatian provenance.

Then there is Muscadet. Muscadet is made from the grape variety called Muscadet in fact, although when it was grown elsewhere in France, it used to be called the *melon blanc*. But is anyone showing the slightest interest in growing *melon blanc* elsewhere? If you have tasted any Muscadet recently, you know the answer to this question and you are right to assume that there isn't a wine-grower in the entire planet who gives a brass farthing for *melon blanc*. (Actually there is one with some affection for it at least: Daniel Gehrs of Santa Cruz California. Mr Gehrs is a grower in a million but I've never tasted his wine.) It is a great shame *melon blanc* has gone the way of the dog-cart and hand-milking. Thirty years ago flavoursome, melon-fruity, mineral-crisp Muscadets were the norm, not the exception as they are today. And any New World wine-grower who tasted them would have said, 'I'd like to grow wine which tastes like that.'

Viognier was once the exclusive grape of a small area of the Rhône, likewise Chenin Blanc in the Loire. Verdelho was strictly Portuguese, kept for making madeiras in the eponymous island. But Australian Viogniers, not to mention those from Languedoc-Roussillon, are much more exciting than most of the Rhône examples, and they are cheaper. In South Africa, Chenin Blanc gets called Steen, but it's the same grape and much fruitier grown in the Cape than in the Rhône. In Western Australia, Verdelho turns out scrumptiously fruity wines some of which are stunningly complex and delicious. In Hawkes Bay, in New Zealand, Chenin Blanc can also be grown to full, rich, complex effect.

But the most famous French region associated with particular grape varieties is Burgundy, where the whites are all Chardonnay and the reds all Pinot Noir. Or rather it is widely believed there are only two permitted varieties in the region, but *Aligote* is used to make certain white wines and even Pinot Blanc puts in the odd appearance (Adnams has an interesting Rully in this connection, vastly overpriced at £12.65 but interesting, called **Gresigny** from Domaine Cogny), and Gamay is regularly blended with Pinot Noir to create a marriage called *passe-tout-grains*. Nevertheless, in the popular imagination, whatever that might be when it's at home, Chardonnay and Pinot Noir are Burgundy's great gifts to the world. Yet as anyone who has ever tasted a Chardonnay from the Hunter Valley in New South Wales or a smelly old Pinot Noir from Washington State or Oregon will attest, Burgundy no longer turns out the smartest examples of the breed. At one time, Burgundy's wines were incomparable. But wonderful examples in this day and age are rarer than female professional footballers.

Thus far, the New World has hung on to its few unique grapes without creating a huge 'me-too' backlash. But then the New World of wine hasn't been at it for very long, indeed no time at all compared with France and Germany (whose Riesling is being turned into a brilliantly fruity, unsweet wine in so many New World areas). So it's very early days yet.

There are three red grape varieties which are intimately associated with particular regions of the new wine world and, thus far, no one has managed to copy them at their finest. But there are growers and wine-makers who have tried and are still trying. These varieties are Pinotage in South Africa, Shiraz in Australia, and Zinfandel in California. However, it is interesting to note – before Zin takes centre stage – that Pinotage has been grown in California and made into wine by an impressive fellow called Kent Rasmussen. Alas, when I sat in his garage and tasted his Pinotage and exclaimed how delicious it was, he calmly informed me that I should make the most of it because it would be the last anyone would see or taste from California for quite some time. 'The vineyard which grew this wine,' he informed me, stroking a beard as capacious as that from which the gentleman in the Edward Lear limerick produced two larks and a wren, two owls and a hen, 'is no longer with us. Phylloxera, the vine pest, got into the vines and the grower has grubbed up everything to prevent it spreading to his other plants. It was the last Pinotage vineyard in California.'

As it happens, a well-formed, well-roasted hen would have gone brilliantly with Kent's Pinotage, and quite the same sort of fowl would suit Italy's excellent Shiraz (called **Casale del Giglio**, £3.49 at Tesco) as well as the Zinfandel grown in Chile. However, no one yet grows Shiraz as blisteringly fulsome and well-textured as that grown in Australia, no one has yet turned Pinotage into a world-class wine like the Cape's wine-growers, and Zinfandel, made into a rich, leathery, aromatic monster of huge flavour and potency, is the preserve of America's richest State and no one has yet created such complex wines from it as the Californians. True, Zinfandel can be a pale rosé, called white Zin, but we are not concerned with it in this abominable and wishy-washy state, we are only interested in the grape in its rich, red manifestation. If anyone can copy it, it ought to be the southern Italians, for it is from here that the Zinfandel vine is said to have originated – sprung from the local variety called *primitivo.*

But in the final analysis, Zinfandel for me is one winery's expression of one vineyard: Ridge Paso Robles. It is a Californian winery I have never visited. But the wine I have visited many times, ever since it first visited me in 1980 when I discovered it in a bar in New York and a bomb went off under my tongue.

Ridge is a Japanese-owned winery nowadays, no doubt run by silken-suited men who house their ready cash between slivers of dead reptile, so maybe the place isn't the same any more (though I think the wine itself is better than when I first tasted it fifteen years ago). But then I recall the time, a couple of years back, when I found myself sitting down to a restaurant dinner with Chris Kelly, the ringmaster of the Gilly and Oz show (*excuse me,* I mean BBC TV's *Food and Drink* programme), and his wife. There on the wine list was **Ridge Paso Robles Zinfandel 1987**, and the Kellys' faces when they tasted this wine for the first time were like those of a couple just delivered of their firstborn. I can also remember the time I handed a glass of the Ridge 1990 to a wealthy wine nut who thought £100 bottles of bordeaux were the only wines in the world, and he fell over backwards into his prejudices when he tasted the wine. Another Ridge Zinfandel, **Lytton Springs 1992**, is also a lovely wine, with stunning aroma, body and depth, and Oddbins were selling it at around fifteen quid the bottle in the spring of '96.

You know what I'm drinking while I write this? I'll tell you. I am being slightly unfaithful to my romantic notions. It was a Christmas present last year: a dozen half-bottles of **Ridge Santa Cruz Mountain Cabernet 1992**. Yes, Cabernet, not Zinfandel. It costs all of £7 or so for the half-bottle at Majestic Wine Warehouses but I cannot persuade myself that I am undeserving of the luxury or indeed should feel embarrassed by the necessity to flirt with other members of the Ridge family. Do I need to travel to the Santa Cruz mountains in the San Francisco Bay area to unearth the secret of Ridge vineyards, whatever the grape variety? All I need, when all is said and done, is a corkscrew.

POSTSCRIPT: THE SCIENTIST, THE TERROIR-IST AND THE PHILOSOPHER

In the end, I had only to jump on my bike and cycle across London and down to the Thames to get closer acquainted with Ridge. I sat and listened to Ridge's wine-maker, Paul Draper, talk about his wines at a seminar organized by the Institute of Masters of Wine at the Royal Festival Hall on the South Bank. Brian Croser (the scientist) talked about his Coonawarra Cabernets as though they were created in a laboratory, Peter Sichel (the *terroir*-ist) talked about how his Cabernet-dominated Chateau Palmer, a famous Margaux vineyard of legendary reputation and status in Bordeaux, owed everything to the soil and the mesoclimate of the vineyard, and Paul Draper (who trained as a philosopher) talked about history and geology and, most interesting of all, his refusal to accept the argument that all the character of a wine comes from its grape. He said: 'I wish it was true that the character of the wine comes from the grape. But I live in the New World and the vast majority of producers believe that by using different vineyards they are creating the wine at the tasting table. The fact is that *they* are manufacturing the character of the wine.' In other words, people make wine – NOT the grape, NOT the vineyard site, NOT centuries of myth. This is why wine from a so-called great vineyard is often poor and wine from a vineyard with no reputation whatsoever is wonderful. Mr Draper's **Ridge Monte Bello Santa Cruz Cabernet** was eloquent proof of that at this seminar because it knocked the French wine into a cocked hat. I wasn't surprised.

I was surprised, however, to find a reflective, middle-aged American male. America has made such an icon out of youth and a science from senility that a wine-maker who fits neither category, and who hankers after the European spirit, must feel a fish out of water. But then Ridge wines are an exception too.

Will the day come when I'll visit Santa Cruz and officially slip the ring on Ridge's finger? Maybe. Some love affairs, as Byron so cutely and perhaps cynically observed, require permanent distance to lend the view enchantment, and the best view of Ridge, whether it is the Cabernet or especially if it's the Zinfandel, has to be two inches from the end of the nose, glinting purple in the glass. I shall leave it like that for now.

Unless, of course, I can persuade the producer of the TV series that we *have* to film at Ridge…

STOCKISTS AND SUPPLIERS:

Adnams
The Crown
High Street
Southwold
Suffolk
Tel 01502 727220
Fax 01502 727223

Asda Stores Ltd
Asda House
Great Wilson Street
Leeds LS11 5AD
Tel 0113 2435435
Fax 0113 2418146

Averys
7 Park Street
Bristol BS1 5NG
Tel 0117 9214141
Fax 0117 922729

Bentalls
Anstee House
Wood Street
Kingston upon Thames
Surrey KT1 1TX
Tel 0181 546 2002

Berry Bros & Rudd
3 St James's Street
London SW1A 1EG
Tel 0171 396 9600
Fax 0171 396 9611

E H Booth & Co Ltd
4-6 Fishergate
Preston
Lancashire PR1 3LJ
Tel 01772 251701
Fax 01772 204316

Budgens Stores Ltd
PO Box 9
Stonefield Way
Ruislip
Middlesex HA4 0JR
Tel 0181 422 9511
Fax 0181 422 1596

Co-op Wholesale Society
PO Box 53
New Century House
Manchester M60 4ES
Tel 0161 834 1212
Fax 0161 834 4507

Connolly's
Arch 13
220 Livery Street
Birmingham B3 1EU
Tel 0121 236 9269
Fax 0121 233 2339

Corney & Barrow
12 Helmet Row
London EC1V 3QJ
Tel 0171 251 4051

Davisons Wine Merchants
7 Aberdeen Road
Croydon
Surrey CR0 1EQ
Tel 0181 681 3222
Fax 0181 760 0390

Direct Wine Shipments
5-7 Corporation Square
Belfast
Northern Ireland BT1 3AJ
Tel 01232 243906
Fax 01232 240202

Eldridge Pope & Co
Weymouth Avenue
Dorchester
Dorset DT1 1QT
Tel 01305 251251
Mail order 0800 378757

John E Fells & Sons
Birkbeck Grove
London W3
Tel 0181 749 3661

Fortnum & Mason
181 Piccadilly
London W1A 1ER
Tel 0171 734 8040

Fuller Smith & Turner plc
Griffin Brewery
Chiswick Lane South
London W4 2BQ
Tel 0181 996 2000
Fax 0181 995 0230

Great Western Wine Co
The Wine Warehouse
Wells Road
Bath BA2 3AP
Tel 01225 448428
Fax 01225 442139

Harrods
Knightsbridge
London SW1X 7QX
Tel 0171 730 1234
Harvey Nichols
Knightsbridge
London SW1X 7RJ
Tel 0171 235 5000

King & Barnes
16 Bishopric
Horsham
West Sussex RH12 1QP
Tel 01403 270870
Fax 01403 270570

Kwik Save Stores Ltd
Warren Drive
Prestatyn
Clwyd LL19 7HU
Tel 01745 887111
Fax 01745 882504

Lay & Wheeler
6 Culver Street West
Colchester
Essex CO1 1JA
Tel 01206 764446
Fax 01206 560002

Laymont & Shaw
The Old Chapel
Millpool
Truro
Cornwall TR1 1EX
Tel 01872 70545
Fax 01872 223005

Lea and Sandeman
301 Fulham Road
London SW10 9QH
Tel 0171 376 4767
Fax 0171 351 0275

Littlewoods Stores
Support Centre
Atlantic Pavilion
Albert Dock
Liverpool L70 1AD
Tel 0151 242 6000
Fax 0151 242 6390

London Wine
Chelsea Wharf
15 Lots Road
London SW10 0QF
Tel 0171 351 6856
Mail order 0800 581266

Majestic Wine
Warehouses
Odhams Trading Estate
St Albans Road
Watford
Hertfordshire WD2 5RE
Tel 01923 816999
Fax 01923 819105

Marks & Spencer
Michael House
57 Baker Street
London W1A 1DN
Tel 0171 935 4422
Fax 0171 487 2679

Wm Morrison
Supermarkets
Wakefield 41 Industrial
Estate
Wakefield
West Yorkshire WF1 0XF
Tel 01924 870000
Fax 01924 821250

The Nobody Inn
Doddiscombsleigh
Nr Exeter
Devon EX5 7PS
Tel 01647 52394
Fax 01647 52978

Oddbins
31-21 Weir Road
Wimbledon
London SW19 8UG
Tel 0181 944 4400
Fax 0181 944 4411

Peckham and Rye
21 Clarence Drive
Hyndland
Glasgow G12 9QN
Tel 0141 334 4312

Playford Ros
Middle Park House
Sowerby
Thirsk
North Yorkshire
YO7 3AH
Tel 01845 526777
Fax 01845 526888

Safeway plc
Safeway House
6 Millington Road
Hayes UB3 4AY
Tel 0181 848 8744
Fax 0181 573 1865

J Sainsbury plc
Stamford House
Stamford Street
London SE1 9LL
Tel 0171 921 6000
Fax 0171 921 7608

Selfridges
400 Oxford Street
London W1A 1AB
Tel 0171 629 1234

Somerfield
Gateway House
Hawkfield Business Park
Whitchurch Lane
Bristol BS14 0TJ
Tel 0117 9359359
Fax 0117 0780629

Spar Landmark
32-40 Headstone Road
Harrow
Middlesex HA3 5QT
Tel 0181 863 5511
Fax 0181 863 0603

Stratfords Wine Shippers
The Old Butcher's Wine
Cellar
High Street
Cookham
Berkshire SL6 9SQ
Tel 01628 810606
Fax 01628 810605

T & W Wines
51 King Street
Thetford
Norfolk IP24 2AU
Tel 01842 765646

Tanners
26 Wyle Cop
Shrewsbury
Shropshire SY1 1XD
Tel 01743 232400

Tesco
Tesco House
PO Box 18 Delamare
Road
Cheshunt EN8 9SL
Tel 01992 632222
Fax 01992 644235

Thresher/Wine
Rack/Bottoms Up
Sefton House
42 Church Road
Welwyn Garden City
Hertfordshire AL8 6PJ
Tel 01707 328344
Fax 01707 371398

Unwins Wine Group Ltd
Birchwood House
Victoria Road
Dartford
Kent DA1 5AJ
Tel 01322 272711
Fax 01322 294469

Valvona & Crolla
19 Elm Row
Edinburgh EH7 4AA
Tel 0131 556 6066

Victoria Wine Company
Dukes Court
Duke Street
Woking
Surrey GU21 5XL
Tel 01483 715066
Fax 01483 755234

Vintage Roots
Sheeplands Farm
Wargrave Road
Wargrave
Berkshire RG10 8DT
Tel 01734 401222
Fax 01734 404814

Waitrose Ltd
Customer Service
Department
Southern Industrial Area
Bracknell
Berkshire RG12 8YA
Tel 01344 424680
Fax 01344 862584

Weavers of Nottingham
Vintner House
1 Castle Gate
Nottingham
Nottinghamshire
NG1 7AQ
Tel 0115 9580922
Fax 0115 9508076

Wine Cellar
PO Box 476
Loushers Lane
Warrington WA4 6RR
Tel 01925 444555
Fax 01925 415474

The Wine Society
Gunnells Wood Road
Stevenage
Hertfordshire SG1 2BG
Tel 01438 741177
Fax 01438 741392

WINES FEATURED IN THE TELEVISION SERIES

This is not an exhaustive list of the wines featured in the television series, but it does represent the great majority of the wines covered. In order to make the series as contemporary as possible, and to ensure that the wines would be widely on sale when each programme was transmitted, certain brilliant wines clamoured to be included in the late summer/early autumn of 1996. By then, of course, this book was already in the tender hands of its printer, but how could I resist putting these wonderful wines on the box? What this means is that some wines in the television series do not appear in the main body of this book (though they may be in the list below). I have explained certain reasons for the impossibility of a perfect world existing where wine is concerned in the Health Warning at the front of this book, but one reason I omitted was the all-embracing thirst of a wine writer unable to restrain his passion for wines discovered rather late in the day. Television, of course, can to some extent cope with such tardiness, but printers and book publishers, alas, cannot; however adroit these generous souls are, distribution of the precious tome to thousands of bookshops must take place even whilst the television producer is still fiddling with her camera and shouting at her presenter.

PROGRAMME 1

WINE	SHOPS/AVAILABILITY	PRICE
Tesco own-label Grenache	all stores	£2.99
Domaine de la Cessane Grenache Syrah 1993	Sainsbury – some stores	£6.45
Don Darias Red	Asda – all stores; Bottoms Up – all stores; Safeway – some stores; Thresher – all stores; Victoria Wine – all stores; Wine Rack – all stores	£2.99 – £3.49
Sicilian Rosso	Asda – all stores	£2.89
Co-op own-label Chardonnay	Co-op – all stores	£4.49
Joao Pires Muscat 1995	Co-op – some stores; Fullers – all stores; Majestic – all stores; Tesco – some stores	£4.29 – £4.49
Three Choirs Estate Premium Medium Dry 1994	Morrisons – all stores; Sainsbury – some stores; Tesco – some stores; Thresher; Waitrose – some stores	£3.99 – £4.45

PROGRAMME 2

Palacio de la Vega Merlot Navarra	Oddbins – all stores (1993)	£5.99
Jackson Estate Sauvignon Blanc 1995	Davisons – some stores; Oddbins – all stores	£7.99 – £8.99

Chateau Reynella Basket Pressed Shiraz 1994	Asda – all stores; Berkeley Wines – all stores; Fullers – all stores; Waitrose – some stores; Wine Cellar – all stores	£7.99
Chateau Reynella Chardonnay 1995	Asda – all stores	£7.99
Mas Segala Red 1995	Asda – all stores	£3.99
Moroccan Cabernet Sauvignon Syrah 1995	Morrisons – all stores	£3.39
Woodford Hill Dry White 1996	Oddbins – all stores	£3.19
Devil's Rock Riesling 1994 or 1995	Asda – all stores; Co-op – some stores; Morrisons – all stores; Sainsbury –some stores; Tesco – all stores; Waitrose – all stores	£3.49 – £3.99
Gran Calesa Costers del Segre 1992	Marks & Spencer	£5.49

PROGRAMME 4

Penfolds Bin 2 Shiraz/ Mourvedre 1994	Sainsbury – some stores; Oddbins –/ all stores	£5.49
Namaqua South African White (3 litre box)	Safeway – all stores	£12.99
Chateau Michelet Red (2 litre box)	Tesco – some stores	£9.99

PROGRAMME 5

Tesco own-label Montilla Dry Sherry	some stores	£3.49
Daniel le Brun Sparkling Wine	Fortnum & Mason; Harvey Nichols; Harrods	£12.99
Montana Lindauer Brut Sparkling White	Asda – all stores; Bottoms Up – all stores; Co-op – some stores; Oddbins – all stores; Safeway – some stores; Sainsbury – some stores; Tesco –some stores; Thresher – all stores; Victoria Wine – all stores; Waitrose – allstores; Wine Rack – all stores	£6.99 – £7.49
Sainsbury's Hungarian Cabernet Sauvignon Rosé	all stores	£3.25

PROGRAMME 6

Le Trulle Negroamaro del Salento 1994	Majestic – all stores	£3.99
Guelbenzu Navarra 1994	Majestic – all stores	£5.99
Seppelt Great Western Brut Rosé	Thresher – all stores	£4.99
Santara Chardonnay 1995	Oddbins – all stores	£3.99
Varichon et Clerc Blanc de Blanc (NV) Extra Dry	Adnams; Lay & Wheeler; Tanners; Unwins	£7.33

GAZETTEER

(places and vineyards)

INDEX